The Nine Degrees of Autism

The Nine Degrees of Autism presents a much-needed positive tool for understanding the developmental process of autism, and to facilitate the improved mental health and well-being of individuals on the spectrum. The ground-breaking model charts nine distinct stages of development – from pre-identification, to learning to live with changes in self-image following a late diagnosis, through to self-acceptance and well-being. Using the model as a framework each chapter focuses on a particular stage of the process. Experts provide personal insights into the environmental and societal challenges faced by individuals with autism, and dispel a number of popular misconceptions.

The positive developmental model described in this book will encourage people on the spectrum to accept themselves by focusing on their gifts rather than weaknesses, and to avoid identifying with negative medical classifications. The developmental process which the authors describe is also applicable to other "hidden" neurological conditions such as dyslexia, dyspraxia, aphasia, and ADHD.

The book should be read by anyone who wants to understand the real nature and experience of autism and will also be essential reading for a range of professionals seeking to work more effectively with individuals on the spectrum.

Philip Wylie is a freelance writer, researcher, and independent management consultant who was diagnosed with Asperger's syndrome in 2013. He conceived The Nine Degrees of Autism during his identity alignment process while writing a book about very late diagnosis of Asperger's syndrome.

Wenn B. Lawson is a researcher, psychologist, writer, and poet with high-functioning autism. He has operated his own private practice for more than 20 years and written several books and research articles on the topic.

Luke Beardon is a Senior Lecturer at The Autism Centre at Sheffield Hallam University, UK. He has worked for several years in the fields of autism and Asperger's syndrome, in capacities ranging from practitioner to researcher and trainer.

The Nine Degrees of Autism
A Developmental Model for the Alignment and Reconciliation of Hidden Neurological Conditions

Philip Wylie, Wenn B. Lawson, and Luke Beardon

Routledge
Taylor & Francis Group

LONDON AND NEW YORK

First published 2016
by Routledge
27 Church Road, Hove, East Sussex BN3 2FA

and by Routledge
711 Third Avenue, New York, NY 10017

Routledge is an imprint of the Taylor & Francis Group, an informa business

British Library Cataloguing in Publication Data
A catalogue record for this book is available from the British Library

Library of Congress Cataloging-in-Publication Data
The nine degrees of autism : a developmental model for the
    alignment and reconciliation of hidden neurological
    conditions / [edited by] Philip Wylie, Wenn B. Lawson
    and Luke Beardon.
        p. ; cm.
    Includes bibliographical references and index.
  I. Wylie, Philip, 1960– , editor. II. Lawson, Wendy,
1952– , editor. III. Beardon, Luke, editor.
  [DNLM: 1. Child Development Disorders, Pervasive—
complications. 2. Adult. 3. Mental Disorders.
4. Social Identification. WM 203.5]
  RC553.A88
  616.85'882—dc23
  2015006897

ISBN: 978-1-138-88716-9 (hbk)
ISBN: 978-1-138-88717-6 (pbk)
ISBN: 978-1-315-71433-2 (ebk)

Typeset in Times and Frutiger
by Apex CoVantage, LLC

Printed by Ashford Colour Press Ltd., Gosport, Hampshire.

Contents

List of contributors

TONY ATTWOOD PhD (Aus): Clinical Psychologist specializing in Autism

Professor Tony Attwood is a clinical psychologist who has specialized in autism spectrum conditions (ASC), and especially Asperger's syndrome, for over 30 years. He is an adjunct professor at Griffith University and is the chairperson at the Minds and Hearts clinic in Brisbane (www.mindsandhearts.net). He works as a clinician and is the author of several books on Asperger's syndrome, including *Asperger's Syndrome: A Guide for Parents and Professionals*, which has sold over 400,000 copies and *The Complete Guide to Asperger's Syndrome*. His web address is www.tonyattwood.com.au

LAURA BATTLES MEd (UK): Autism Specialist and Director of Family and Caregiver Support

Laura has worked in the field of autism and additional support needs for the past 20 years as a teacher, manager, and as Director of Autism Services. More recently, she worked as a private consultant in the United Arab Emirates and now she is undertaking the role of Director of Family and Caregiver Support at The Developing Child Centre in Dubai. Laura has also worked for the National Autistic Society in Autism Accreditation as a team leader and panel member reviewing standards of practice within schools, and services across the United

Kingdom. She studied autism and additional support needs extensively and is currently studying for a Doctorate of Education at Stirling University.

LUKE BEARDON EdD (UK): Senior Lecturer in Autism at Sheffield Hallam University

Luke Beardon BA (Hons), PG Cert (Autism), EdD is a senior lecturer in autism at Sheffield Hallam University. He has worked with the National Autistic Society as a trainer and consultant, as well as a service coordinator in residential services, helping young autistic adults to access suitable residential services. Luke works in various capacities, from consultant to researcher and trainer. He has also written, edited, and provided forewords for several publications about autism and Asperger's syndrome. He is also a registered expert witness (see www.the-expert-witness.co.uk/luke-beardon). His doctor of education thesis was on *Asperger Syndrome and Perceived Offending Conduct*.

EMILY L. CASANOVA PhD (USA)

Dr. Emily L. Casanova has a PhD in Anatomy and Neurobiology, specializing in developmental, cellular, and molecular biology, with a focus in neuroscience. Her work utilizes a combination of bioinformatics and benchtop techniques. Her primary foci are the study of autism, intellectual disability, and schizophrenia, but she has also studied neuroectoderm development and cancers of the epidermis. In the study of neurodevelopmental conditions, she has used a combination of in vivo models and bioinformatics techniques. Her bioinformatics work has been two-pronged: (1) to investigate the functional overlap of high-risk autism genes; and (2) to characterize genomic features common to autism-risk, schizophrenia-risk, and central nervous system–related genes.

MANUAL F. CASANOVA MD (USA): Professor of Psychiatry at the University of Louisville

Dr. Manuel F. Casanova is the Gottfried and Gisela Kolb Endowed Chair in Psychiatry at the University of Louisville. At present he shares appointments within the Departments of Psychiatry, Neurology, Anatomy, and Bioengineering. He serves as an editor for 15 journals and has published over 230 refereed articles and 72 book chapters. Among other honors he was a plenary speaker at the World Congress of Autism, a recipient of an EUREKA award from the NIMH, a Stanley Scholar, and holds a honorary doctoral degree from the University of Krasnoyarsk.

MICHAEL FITZGERALD PhD (EIRE): Henry Marsh Professor at Trinity College Dublin

Prof. Michael Fitzgerald is Henry Marsh Professor of Child and Adolescent Psychiatry at Trinity College Dublin. He was the first professor of child psychiatry in Ireland in 1996. He has a doctorate in autism. He trained at St. Patrick's Hospital Dublin, Chicago Medical School, and the Maudsley Hospital. He has clinically diagnosed over 2,600 individuals with autism and Asperger's syndrome and has served on the Government Task Force on Autism and the Family. Michael Fitzgerald's website address is: www.professormichaelfitzgerald.eu

TEMPLE GRANDIN PhD (USA): Professor of Animal Science at Colorado State University

Temple Grandin is a professor of animal sciences at Colorado State University where she continues her research while teaching courses on livestock handling and facility design. She is also an internationally renowned speaker at autism conferences and she has authored the following books: *Emergence: Labeled Autistic*; *Thinking in Pictures: My Life with Autism*; *Different . . . Not Less*; *The Way I See It: A Personal Look at Autism and Asperger's*; *The Autistic Brain: Thinking Across the Spectrum*.

SARA HEATH MEd (UK): Asperger's Syndrome Facilitator, Mentor, and Consultant

Sara Heath MEd, who is a believer in the social model of disability, established Autonomy (see www.shropshireautonomy.co.uk), an Asperger's self-help group based in Shropshire, and runs it with her son Eric. Sara is also a practitioner at AutonomyPlus+, an Asperger-specific consultancy, where she provides pre-diagnostic assessments and reports for people on the autism spectrum, as well as post-diagnostic support services. Sara interviewed the survey respondents – who are all national or local members of Autonomy – for the *Very Late Diagnosis of Asperger's Syndrome (ASC) 2013 UK Survey*, which she published jointly with Philip Wylie.

WENN B. LAWSON PhD CPsychologist BSc (UK) MAPS (Aus): Autism Researcher and Lecturer, Psychologist, and Writer

Dr. Wenn B. Lawson CPsychol MAPS, researcher, psychologist, writer, and poet has operated his own private practice for more than 20 years. Wenn was awarded fourth place as "Victorian Australian of the Year" in 2008. Originally diagnosed as being intellectually disabled, then in his teens as being schizophrenic, and finally in 1994, Wenn was diagnosed as being on the autism spectrum. The parent of four children, two of his sons are also on the autistic spectrum. Wenn is passionate about the rights of those who so often cannot speak for themselves and aims to promote justice and equality for all. Wenn has written the following books: *Autism and Ageing* (2015); *The Passionate Mind: How People with Autism Learn* (2011); *Concepts of Normality: The Autistic and Typical Spectrum* (2008); *Friendships the Aspie Way* (2007); *Sex, Sexuality and the Autism Spectrum* (2005); *Build Your Own Life: A Self-Help Guide for Individuals with Asperger's Syndrome* (2003); *Understanding and Working with the Spectrum of Autism: An Insider's View* (2001); and *Life Behind Glass* (2000). Wenn also writes books for children with autism, to help build understanding of the confusing world we all live in.

DEBRA MOORE PhD (USA): Psychologist and Founder and Former Director of Fall Creek Counseling Associates

Dr. Debra Moore is a psychologist who founded and directed Fall Creek Counseling Associates, a group private practice and approved training site for psychology interns and postdoctoral fellows since the early 1980s. She has recently retired to focus on writing and consulting, with a specialty in autism spectrum disorders. Dr. Moore's goal has been to provide a high standard of psychotherapy and consultation, to educate the public about psychology and mental health through her writings and public speaking, and to provide quality training to interns. She is also the online facilitator of LinkedtoAspergers, Aspie Teens, and Asperger's Helping Hands Mentors.

LOUISE PAGE (Aus): Professional Autism Counselor and Mentor

Louise Page specializes in counseling and advocacy for parents, carers, and individuals living on the autism spectrum. Louise is also an avid writer and author of several books and articles on the subject of Asperger's syndrome, including "An Autism Connection – sharing the journey with other parents." She is a qualified member of both the Australian Institute of Professional Counselling and the Australian Counselling Association. Since 2008, Louise has been providing professional counseling and mentoring support for parents and individuals living with autism in Melbourne, Australia.

ALTAZAR ROSSITER PhD (UK): Holistic Facilitator and Life Coach

Altazar Rossiter is a shamanic "healer" who provides coaching programs, workshops, and consultations for developing spiritual and emotional intelligence (see www.altazarrossiter.com). Altazar's doctorate is in Semiotics, which covers symbolism and psychoanalytic theory. His book is entitled, *Developing Spiritual Intelligence: The Power of You*, which was published by O Books in 2006. Altazar believes that we are all here for a purpose, so he is passionate about enabling his clients to find their own way – whether that fits the norm of the social order or not – and to be at peace with themselves in their unique way. Altazar's website address is: www.altazarrossiter.com

STEPHEN SHORE PhD (USA): Professor of Autism at Adelphi University

Stephen teaches courses in autism spectrum disorders and conducts research into autism at Adelphi University. Stephen served on the Editorial Committee of the Autism File Trust for seven years and developed policy for the Autism Society of America for nine years. Between 1999 and 2010, Stephen was Executive Director of Autism Spectrum Disorders Consulting. He also served as President Emeritus of the Asperger's Association of New England (AANE) for six years. Stephen authored the following books (all published by AAPC): *Beyond the Wall: Personal Experiences with Autism and Asperger Syndrome*; *Ask and Tell: Self-advocacy and Disclosure for People on the Autism Spectrum*; *Living Along the Autism Spectrum: What It*

Means to Have Autism or Asperger Syndrome (DVD). Stephen's website address is http://www.autismexpertshore.com

Other acknowledgments

The editors would like to acknowledge and thank the following autism specialists (listed in alphabetical order) for their contributions in this publication: Maxine Aston, Simon Baron-Cohen, Michael John Carley, Irene Jenks, Leo Gregory, Liane Holliday-Wiley, Rod Morris, Christa Wilson, and Rod Wintour.

Editor Forewords

1. Foreword by Wenn B. Lawson

Autism is experienced differently by each individual. However, there are a number of elements that we each have in common. Our brains are configured to work best with single focus, most of us find eye contact difficult, a number of us live with sensory dysphoria, and the social world is an enigma to us.

Autism is considered a spectrum of varying ability. Some of us are said to be at the high-functioning end (the term "Asperger's syndrome," although no longer located in the diagnostic manual (*DSM-V*), has been used to describe this group). Others are at the opposite end of the spectrum, are probably living with intellectual disability too and find language very difficult to process. Of course there are many others in the middle and all of us move along the spectrum over time.

Many individuals, though not speaking as children, develop speech as they get older. Lots of us have other comorbid conditions such as attention deficits, learning difficulties (e.g., dyslexia, dyspraxia), epilepsy, eating disorders, or other mental health issues. Wherever an individual is on the autism spectrum, though, this book helps to explain the journey.

The Nine Degrees of Autism is a book unlike any other. It follows a particular developmental model showing nine degrees or stages of autism that build self-esteem, use the positive attributes of the individual, and demonstrate the creation of a spectrum of ability. Although I've used the word "stages," nine degrees is not a forgone or automatic conclusion. Individuals may linger in particular places at varying degrees of autism being pulled or pushed in ways that typical individuals may never experience.

This book depicts a life journey with autism that begins at birth and takes the individual from a place of innocence and naïvety to that of confusion, sensory overload, immense fear, gradual understanding, eventual autonomy, and ultimately to that of selfless giving and legacy projects that benefit humanity.

The Nine Degrees of Autism is a developmental model that clearly and beautifully illustrates a social model of autism allowing individuals to find who they are, where they belong, and how to, not only avoid mental health issues, but positively build a self-esteem that enables them to bless others. This model flies in the face of traditional explanations of autism that state if an individual is autistic that person lacks empathy, is self-focused, inward-looking, and not capable of acts of love or selfless giving.

The idea that autistic individuals lack "theory of mind" and are not able to appreciate another's point of view is questionable. What we know about autism is that we are single-minded and this, by definition, means we may not notice or connect to what is happening for others. This is not lack of ability to notice but ability that is focused elsewhere. When others engage with us via our passions and particular interests, they open doors to connection that otherwise remain closed.

This simple act of appreciating how our brains work is the key that unlocks self and other sharing that is not otherwise negotiated. The chapters in this book show the development to connection and the challenge to own one's true identity. To face the pain and confusion of not fitting in, travel through the forest of falsehood and masked greenery to take on the ability to blend, then realize these are the Emperor's new clothes and their covering is superficial and not real. To own this, admit to one's true identity, and build a present that leads to a future one can be proud of takes courage and commitment.

Nine Degrees offers its readers a clear landscape of what to expect and when. It makes no bones about the difficulties, the hardships, or the joys of such a journey. It does not presume to know anyone's story in particular or usurp any other authority. It simply tells it like it is.

The choice is left to the reader. Will you join us upon this journey and acknowledge the truth of your experience (third, fourth, fifth, and sixth degree of autism)? Will you move beyond your well-worn, but forged identity (the one you let others see) or will you stay in hiding where you believe it's safe? Ultimately you could be living in a place, despite your circumstances, where you take control of your life rather than continuing to let it control you.

Nine Degrees not only shows you the journey for autism awareness, acceptance, and the way forward, it offers an explanation of where you've come from and why. Our pasts so often determine our present and our future. The thing that haunts us most, though, is the lack of control we seem to have and how easily our processing of information leaves us wanting. This could mean our past dominates and we might miss any opportunity that might open up for us. For example, one of the most difficult things we live with is the time it takes for us in processing what has been said. Others may share information with us, join us in conversation, or point us in a particular direction. But, by the time we've processed what was said and what it might mean, the information may be lost, the conversation moved on, and the direction no longer available.

Autism can lead us to deep frustration, yes. But, on the flip side of this we have an enormous spirit for adventure, an uncanny "knowing" for truth with an "eye" for the authentic, a gift of love and laughter that outstrips adversity and, at times, academic skills that support us in all our research, writing, teaching, and, of course, the gaining of understanding.

It's the flip side of the difficulties autism presents that *Nine Degrees* outlines so well.

This book does not follow the "medical deficit" model for autism. It does not point to ways to "cure" or heal the condition because any sickness either abides in individuals or in the society we inhabit. As autistic individuals, we are not sick and do not need to recover! The thing we need most, as this book demonstrates so well, is to develop understanding as we experience the various degrees of autism. It's not just awareness and acceptance though. This book shows us how to go further and gives us grounds to become all we can be, and then some.

I encourage you, as you read this book, to do so with an open mind and an open heart. Don't judge yourself or others, that's a work that wastes time and energy that could be being channeled into more helpful and healthy pursuits. We know better than this now.

We know how to build up rather than tear down. We know how to encourage and support, rather than criticize and monopolize. This books says you are a free agent, beholden to no one but yourself. Take this opportunity and let it develop you to become the "you" that YOU want for yourself. Don't accept any other offer!

Enjoy the journey, Wenn.

2. Foreword by Luke Beardon

Acknowledgments. To Philip, for making himself known to me and subsequently all the hard work he has made me do! It has been a pleasure. To Wenn, always great to work alongside one of the best in the business. To all the individuals and families who have let me into their lives and shared their experiences with me, I am forever in your debt. To the contributors to the *Nine Degrees* – brilliant job, thank you. To mi amigo – you know who you are. And my own fab three, Fionn, Guy, and Kate – as always, without you I am nothing.

To start – an autism fable

Many moons ago on a planet similar to ours but several light years from us, there lived a colony of ants. These ants were a sociable bunch, and they took their community very seriously indeed. There was a hierarchy of sorts, and the ants all got along with one another, and followed the rules laid down by their parents, who followed the same patterns of behavior as their parents, and so on and on. Some ants were more playful than others, some were more serious; some liked their own company, while others were more outgoing. On the whole, though, all of the ants got along because they shared similar interests, they all mucked in with one another, and they all knew what their roles and responsibilities were.

One day, Annabelle Ant and Angus Ant discovered, much to their delight, that they were expecting their third little antling. They loved their two other antlings, and awaited eagerly the arrival of the newest addition to the family. Soon enough the big day came, and tiny little Annie Ant was introduced to the world. Everyone adored Annie, she was so quiet and caused no fuss; in fact, she seemed to be quite happy simply being – she didn't seem to need much attention, and all was well. Until, that is, she started getting a little older.

Things were not quite as Annabelle and Angus had expected. Their youngest simply didn't seem to be quite the same as the other antlings in the colony; they couldn't really point to any one thing, but there just seemed to be something a bit different. She didn't seem to like chatting, she refused to sleep, she wouldn't dress the same as everyone else, she appeared to be getting more and more defiant as she grew.

At antling school she looked forward to the lessons, but didn't look forward to going out to play at all. This was quite the opposite to what the other antlings experienced. She didn't seem to want to make friends, choosing to practice her ever-evolving complex dance movements on the edge of the antling play area. Occasionally the parents were asked to go into school, as Annie had done something that was apparently egregious, though Annie herself didn't seem to think anything of it. This was bad for the parents . . . but far, far worse for Annie.

Hi, this is Annie's diary. Today at school was the worst ever. As always, I tried my hardest to be invisible. As always, I just seemed to stand out even more. I wanted to cry, but I know this makes everyone look at me and ask me what is wrong – but the point is, I don't know what is wrong, so how am I supposed to answer?

I just want all the horrible feelings to go away, and for the other antlings to leave me alone. I would love just one friend, but every time I try to make a friend something goes horribly wrong, and I either upset them or they laugh at me. Everyone else gets on with one another just fine, I try SO hard to fit in, what is so wrong with me?

Oh, diary, I just don't know what to do. It's as if the others have a rulebook that they follow, but I am not allowed to read it. They just find everything so easy, while I try harder than them but still get things wrong. Every day I set out determined for it to be different; every day I am devastated that yet again I have done something wrong. I can't bear all the attention I bring on myself, but I don't know what else to do. Diary, PLEASE HELP . . .

As we can see, Annie was not in a happy place at all. Her parents loved her but were increasingly worried that they could not seem to connect with their daughter. At school some of the teachers thought she was wonderful and bright, while others found her naughty and poorly behaved. And then, one day, something magical happened.

Annie was in the library as usual; she liked the quiet, the lighting, and ambience. She was forever reading up on ant-ology in case it helped her make sense of the world around her. She noticed what she thought was an error in the spine of a book on the shelf, and grabbed it with annoyance; printing errors should never be published, she thought to herself. *The Trials and Tribulations of Ents* sounded like a great title to her, but everyone knows that there is no such thing as an ent, and it should have read "Ants."

She started reading it out of curiosity, and before she knew it she was spellbound. It turned out that ents *did* exist. They were physically similar to ants, but their way of thinking and processing the world around them was astoundingly different. There were only a few of them compared to the ant population, which sometimes made them feel very lonely. Apparently it was very common for the ant colony to misunderstand the individual ent, making the erroneous assumption that ants were all the same, and not believing in ents at all!

As Annie read, she was hit by a sudden rush in her brain, and she started to cry. For the first time in her life out of relief, not pain. "I'm an ent, not an ant," she whispered to herself. "Ent, not ant. Ent, ent, ent," she murmured, liking the sounds of the words.

She carried on reading, and took the book home with her to study that night. She read every word of the book, and learned all about how other ents lived their lives, what problems they had faced, and why. She read all about how being an ent might put you at a disadvantage, because others may not understand you, but that there is nothing at all wrong with being an ent. She learned that all ents were different, but may share all sorts of similar problems. Annie, for the first time in her life, learned about herself.

* * * * * *

Hi, this is Annie's diary. I graduated today – hurray! Of course I didn't actually go to the graduation, nor the party after, but no one cares about that. All my friends had a good time and sent their best wishes through the post, just as I like it. I can't wait to start my new job! Who would have thought that I am the official teacher in charge of ent-ology at University! I bet none of my teachers ever would have thought that would happen! Mind you, I certainly never thought I would manage to get through school, let alone go to college and end up with a job – and now look at me, I have a lovely select group of friends, a job, and my very own goldfish.

Ha ha to those who thought I would amount to nothing! Hurray for the ent! I wonder sometimes what would have happened if I hadn't found that book, though. I have several copies of it now, to lend out to my ant friends – and I simply love sharing it with the ents I have found along the way. It's a funny old world, the fact that a book literally changed my life is pretty weird. Diary, as you very well know, every single day I thank all that is great and good for giving me the chance to read it. Thank you, thank you, thank you. I love being an ent, and I love being me. Bye for now!

The Nine Degrees of Autism

I hope you enjoyed the fable, and it is a fable. It's not intended to be a synopsis of an alternative view of autism in another world; but there are fairly clear and obvious parallels. Being autistic among the predominant neurotype can be a difficult existence, not always, of course, but often. Anything that can assist the autistic individual to have a better understanding of self and those around him or her is clearly a good thing.

The Nine Degrees of Autism is not the solution to all the problems faced by all autistic people – I doubt that such a tome could ever be written. But if it can provide some support to autistic individuals on their journey toward understanding who they are, then it is surely well worth all the (considerable) effort that the authors and editors have put into it.

Even if just one individual picks up this book and shares a similar experience to Annie the ent, then all that effort would be worth it. Fingers crossed, the impact will be wide reaching, much further than one person – but the sentiment remains the same. I am a firm believer that having a good understanding of self leads to a more positive outlook on life. It can lead to increased levels of self-worth, confidence, and pride for one's self – something that should be afforded to all. I hope and trust that this book will help you and yours achieve your own ninth degree. Thank you for reading.

Preface

Currently our neurotypical society is largely ignorant at best and intolerant at worst of neurological diversity. In addition to what may be an innate discomfort with what is "foreign" or that which we do not understand, we live in a world that generally measures value to society by industrial output or economic contribution. In 1949 Albert Einstein commented, *"This crippling of individuals I consider the worst evil of capitalism."* My hope is that in the future autistic individuals will be better understood, accepted, and valued for our diverse and unique contributions, not simply measured via a default commercial barometer.

The creation of this book can be regarded a victory if it adds to society's broader conceptualization of the potential within autistic individuals. By presenting a developmental model, my aspiration is that both those on the spectrum and others will better appreciate the typical heroic journey of those on the autism spectrum from birth to self-realization.

Creating this book has been an incredible journey and it's a privilege to work with some of the world's leading experts in the field of autism. Our team of editors and contributors really understands autism. They were handpicked with extreme diligence and many are on the autism spectrum.

You may be surprised that many autistic individuals collaborated to disseminate this innovative developmental model that supports the well-being of people who are on the spectrum. So this book, which is a labor of love, brings hope to a misunderstood culture and demonstrates that autistic people can collaborate on legacy projects.

The Nine Degrees of Autism is special in many ways. Both Luke Beardon and Tony Attwood remarked about the "specialness" of the number nine. Certainly, the monks in Thailand like this number. Also, as Wenn Lawson pointed out, the title is aligned with "*the nine degrees of freedom*," which is a statistical measure of options available.

Freedom is the primary goal for many individuals on the autism spectrum. We need freedom to pursue our own interests and to work on meaningful projects, even if they may appear commercially unviable. Also we need the freedom to live independently rather than being controlled, institutionalized, or coerced into doing things against our will.

How I created this model is a long and complex story which I covered in my book, *Psychobiography of a Systemiser* (refer to www.phil.asia for details). However, it was Luke Beardon who recognized the potential of this model and who patiently helped me to develop it into its current state. So, I am indebted to Luke for enabling this book to reach your hands.

During the gestation of this project several events occurred which I would like to share with you. During exchange of contracts with our publisher, Luke disappeared from planet Earth for around 10 weeks. This event turned out to be a well-camouflaged blessing because I realized that we needed another editor, so I engaged Wenn Lawson as co-editor. Shortly afterward, Luke returned from his space mission and our publishing project was back on track again.

While Luke was engaged with his inter-galactic alignment process, I was aligning my identity; and Wenn was undergoing gender alignment. On top of that, Wenn and Luke were consulting, speaking at conferences and traveling.

The concept of "identity alignment" is fundamental to this developmental model. Luke Beardon suggested this term for the process of reconstructing our self-image following self-identification with our hidden neurotype.

The diagram below illustrates the three stages of identity alignment. For many people identity alignment is an "emotional roller coaster" ride though some individuals experience relief, especially

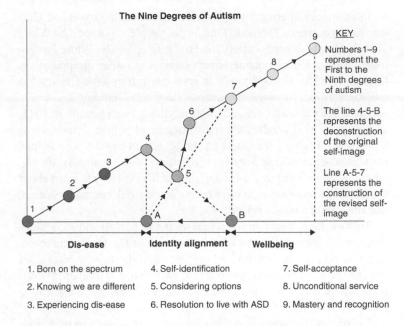

The Nine Degrees of Autism

KEY

Numbers 1–9 represent the First to the Ninth degrees of autism

The line 4-5-B represents the deconstruction of the original self-image

Line A-5-7 represents the construction of the revised self-image

Dis-ease   Identity alignment   Wellbeing

1. Born on the spectrum
2. Knowing we are different
3. Experiencing dis-ease
4. Self-identification
5. Considering options
6. Resolution to live with ASD
7. Self-acceptance
8. Unconditional service
9. Mastery and recognition

following misdiagnoses. In the following chapters you will discover that delay in self-identification can lead to many other health issues too.

My communications with Stephen Shore were fascinating. Each message originated from a different country beginning with Morocco. One message read, "I am not in Nottingham," but he was actually in Nottingham. So I joked, "I am not in Nottingham but I am in Amersham."

There is a 14-hour time difference between the temples in Thailand and Temple Grandin's cattle ranches in Colorado. Naturally, this time difference made it difficult for Temple and me to discuss her role in this project, so Debra Moore kindly agreed to communicate with Temple on my behalf. Chapter 11 (The Ninth Degree of Autism) was written and co-edited exclusively by Temple Grandin and Debra Moore, whereas the rest of the book was co-edited by Wenn, Luke, and myself.

Interestingly, there are two famous temples in a city called Chiang Rai in northern Thailand. One of the temples is called The White Temple and the other is called The Black Temple. The White Temple looks beautiful from outside but its interior is rather disappointing. Conversely, The Black Temple is less interesting superficially but awesome inside. Anyway, my favorite Temple is Grandin!

Just three years ago, I didn't know anything about autism. In 2011, at the age of 51, I reached the fourth degree of autism. Immediately, I contacted a few of the world's leading autism experts who helped me write the guidebook, *Very Late Diagnosis of Asperger's Syndrome*, which was published in 2014. I reckon that the best way to learn about a subject is to connect with top experts in the field, conduct research, and then write a book about it.

This model is based on the social model of autism and recognizes that we are born with autism and we die with the same neurotype. There is no cure for autism and pretending to be neurotypical does not change our neurotype. Moreover, if we live in a favorable environment where diversity is accepted, we can lead productive and happy lives.

There is some notion that this model may also apply to other hidden neurological conditions, such as dyslexia and attention deficit disorder. It's interesting that these conditions overlap and occur more commonly in autism than in the typical population as outlined in Chapter 2 (A Spectrum of Neurodevelopment).

It would also be fair to argue that children's experiences and those of adults diagnosed later in life will be very different. Also most healthcare funding and support is directed toward children, leaving many late-diagnosed adults to struggle alone without any support.

The medical profession is extremely advanced in the field of physical medicine but sadly it knows much less about the mind, especially autism. The medical model of autism focuses on our impairments and encourages "medical and behavioural interventions to address the lack of typical development." These "remedies" are far too short-sighted and fail to consider the "whole person."

This collaborative project is a legacy for the autism community. Autistic people are rarely remembered for what they do in their often neurotypical-controlled "day jobs," but more often for their legacy projects and typically, posthumously. I believe that it is our focus and devotion toward legacy projects (which draw upon our special interests) that enable us to rise up to the *ninth degree of autism,* when we achieve mastery, recognition, and unity. To qualify as a legacy project, the individual must have positive intent to make the world a better place.

The diagram below shows how legacy projects are created: by aligning our talents and abilities with our passionate interests for the benefit of humanity. Now that I have realized my legacy project I would like to encourage and assist others to realize their unique legacy projects.

The critical difference between legacy projects and day jobs is that day jobs can support legacy projects but not usually vice versa. Most legacy projects are risky and many are financially unviable, driven by passionate individuals without thought of future outcome or reward.

A further difference between a legacy project and a typical day job is that people often remember a person for his or her legacy project

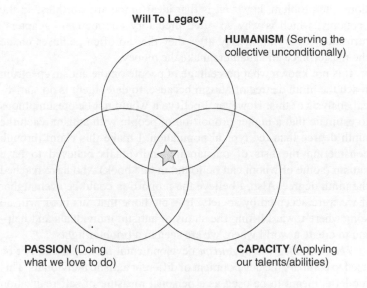

Will To Legacy

HUMANISM (Serving the collective unconditionally)

PASSION (Doing what we love to do)

CAPACITY (Applying our talents/abilities)

 Legacies are created by individuals who follow their heart's desire by applying their talents with intent to benefit humanity

but, unfortunately, rarely for the day job (unless it's also a legacy project). The day job provides the means to continue with the legacy project. The person with a day job is often materializing another person's vision, but not his or her own; and the individual engaged in a legacy project is turning his or her vision into reality. A person who makes the day job the "end game" will most likely not be remembered for a particular service to humanity; although, of course, this is not impossible.

The combination of skill, innate ability, and hard work often enables talent. Genius goes a step further by applying the talent in a different direction, thereby creating something completely different. Genius is driven by passion and is rarely competitive so many masterpieces are valued posthumously.

Arthur Schopenhauer's quote, "Talent hits a target no-one else can hit; Genius hits a target no-one else can see" is most perceptive. Although autistic people – particularly those who have Asperger's syndrome (HFA) – tend to be detail-oriented systematizers, they can also be adept abstract thinkers with immense capacity for innovation. The problem, however, is that ideas alone are worthless in the economy, which is why so often predatory commercial "adapters" turn their ideas into money after they die. So often geniuses create the masterpiece and adapters make the money.

It is not known what percentage of people on the autism spectrum reach the ninth degree of autism because, to date, there is no statistical analysis of this. However, I believe it would not be presumptuous to estimate that a higher proportion of people with autism reach the ninth degree than the typical population. I make this claim through considering the lists of outstanding individuals believed to have autism (some of whom can be found in this book) who have reached the ninth degree. Also, I believe the proportion could be even higher if we were accepted by society. It is my hope that this book will go somewhere toward lifting the status of autistic individuals and helping to create a world where we are seen in a brighter light.

The Nine Degrees of Autism developmental model should not be used to compare the development of different autistic individuals. This model is meant to be used as a personal measure of self-realization only. There are several reasons why it would be inappropriate to compare the progress of different individuals using this system.

Autistic people who reach the ninth degree of autism have success-fully applied their talents in sync with their passion for the benefit of humanity. Everyone has a unique combination of talents and desires, and some individuals may find difficulty integrating their service into society. Therefore a relatively untalented person could reach the ninth degree (if the person accepts himself or herself and finds a way to add value to humanity) whereas a highly talented person may never reach the higher levels due to lack of acceptance by self and society. This model, therefore, falls outside the realm of competition so people should not compare their developmental level with other people who are on the spectrum.

I am concerned that some people may perceive this model as a tool for measuring winners and losers in life. Most autistic people are not competitive but rather ambitious to realize their full potential. Many neurotypical people, on the other hand, seem to have more of a competitive drive hard-wired in them. They may attempt to "win" in games designed by others. However, those on the autistic spectrum are primarily interested in achieving success in arenas they them-selves designed. It is our hope that this developmental model helps them reach that goal.

Thanks for supporting this great project!

Phil Wylie
Chiang Mai
November 2014
www.ninedegrees.pw

Part one
The autism spectrum

1

Introduction

Tony Attwood

The idea for *The Nine Degrees of Autism* was originally conceived by Philip Wylie. The model is consistent with my own observations over four decades as a clinician, during which I have been able to contribute to the development and increasing maturity of several thousand clients of all ages through the many transitions of their lives. Thus, I have had the advantage of a longitudinal perspective of autism. I recognize that for those who are living with autism, there is a "journey" through the lifespan to achieve self-understanding. This introduction is based on my clinical experience and provides a simplified road map to acquire self-acceptance and fulfilment through *The Nine Degrees of Autism*.

The journey is not easy, but is certainly worthwhile. Those contributors to this book who have autism themselves have progressed through the various degrees of autism and write as pathfinders. The other contributors to this book, such as myself, have recognized the nine degrees from their clinical practice. This book will be of great assistance to those who are on the autism spectrum and to their families. Also to other professionals and psychologists, so that we can all be involved in encouraging progression along the journey.

I also hope that the model explored in this book becomes the basis of a new psychotherapy, and that facilitating the journey will reduce mental health issues, encourage feelings of self-worth, and enable those who live with autism to make a significant contribution to society.

The nine degrees

The reader may have autism and recognize that he or she is currently within a specific degree of autism and eager to progress through the remaining degrees; or a family member or professional may want to accelerate their relative's or client's progress along the journey. The following is a brief summary of each degree, with corresponding chapters providing more detailed information on the characteristics of each stage of the journey, and strategies to progress to the next degree.

First degree: being born on the autism spectrum

Autism is not achieved by personal choice, and does not come about as a response to a particular parenting style. The newborn infant who is subsequently diagnosed as having autism has a brain that is wired differently, not defectively. The first person to recognize that the child's development and abilities are different is usually the mother, or primary care giver. She or he observes that the child has:

- a tendency to avoid, or be confused or overwhelmed in, social situations
- a possible motivation to socialize, but difficulty reading body language and social cues
- intense emotions
- an unusual profile of language skills that can include language delay
- different interests to other children of the same age
- difficulty coping with unanticipated changes in routines and expectations
- a sensitivity to specific sensory experiences.

She or he may then try to provide guidance, support, and protection and will probably seek help from a specialist in developmental disorders, leading to a diagnostic assessment. When a child is diagnosed with autism Level 1 (Asperger's syndrome) the signs have usually been recognized in early childhood, often by a teacher who has an understanding of the profile of abilities of a typical child of that age. The teacher perceives that this child is unusual and has a pattern of abilities consistent with the characteristics of being on the autism spectrum.

Sometimes the diagnosis is achieved later in life, during the adolescent or adult years, either because the signs are more subtle or have been deliberately "masked" since early childhood. They may not become apparent to family members, teachers, and clinicians until more complex social demands begin to exceed abilities or coping strategies. There may be the development of a secondary mood or personality disorder; or the adult him- or herself may acquire knowledge on autism, perhaps from the media. Sometimes a relative achieves a diagnosis, and the adult recognizes similarities to his or her own abilities and experiences. Thus the brain is wired differently in utero, but the diagnosis can take many years – even decades – to be formally recognized.

Second degree: knowing you are different

For very young children, the concept of being different to peers is primarily in terms of gender or race. At around six to eight years, children have an increasing recognition of difference in fellow students in terms of abilities, interests, and personality.

It is at this stage of development that the child who is on the autism spectrum recognizes he or she is conspicuously different to peers. This is in terms of interests, social understanding and inclusion, intensity of emotions, and reaction to specific sensory experiences. The child may then question why he or she is not invited to parties, and is rejected when wanting to participate in social play. Other children's interests may be viewed as too complex or boring.

It is at this stage that typical children become natural "child psychologists," having a clear schema of what is typical behavior of children of the same age. They also recognize a qualitative difference between themselves and the child who has autism. This recognition can lead to a change in acceptance of that difference, with some children becoming more compassionate and supportive, while others enjoy isolating, teasing, and ridiculing the child. This latter experience may have a devastating effect on self-esteem and cause the individual to develop secondary physical and mental health issues associated with the third degree of autism.

Third degree: developing secondary physical and mental health problems

There is a range of compensatory and adjustment strategies to being different that may be used by individuals living with autism. Some of these are constructive. Others are destructive in terms of the development of an accurate and positive sense of self, or the development of mental health problems. The strategy used will depend on the individual's personality, experiences, and circumstances.

Those individuals who tend to internalize thoughts and feelings may develop a sense of self-blame and see themselves as defective, leading to the development of a reactive depression. Alternatively, the individual may use imagination and the creation of a fantasy life to escape into another world in which the person is more successful and valued. Those individuals who tend to externalize thoughts and feelings can become arrogant and feel superior to others, who are to be despised and corrected; or they may view others as the solution to the problem of being different, by developing the ability to observe, analyze, and imitate. It is worthwhile further exploring each compensatory or adjustment strategy in terms of the propensity to develop secondary physical and mental health problems.

Depression

Some individuals as young as six years old who have autism may develop signs of depression as a result of their insight into being different, and perceiving difference as a defect. They may not intuitively know how to achieve social inclusion and may lack guidance in how to develop and maintain friendships. This can lead to a crisis in confidence and very low self-esteem. The seeds of a clinical depression may be sown, with the start of negative, pessimistic, or depressive thinking and a belief in the criticisms and derogatory comments of peers.

For those with autism there may be a tendency to experience negative emotions very intensely. In a situation that would be expected to create a relatively mild level of sadness or despair, the person on the autism spectrum may have a catastrophic reaction; I use the term "depression attack." Such a response can be to a situation where the person feels different or defective, and the intensity may be perceived by others as excessive. However, it is very real for the person who is experiencing this. Fortunately, such a "depression attack" is usually short-lived.

When the signs of depression are of clinical significance and become prolonged, there will be a loss of energy, reduced insight into how to cope with life, and, for some, delayed progress to the next phase of the journey. Low self-esteem and periodic depression can last decades or a life time. We urgently need to develop strategies and therapy to alleviate the signs of depression and change negative thinking and feelings of low self-worth. The low mood and energy levels associated with depression can also affect physical health, with a resultant lethargy and a tendency to adopt an unhealthy lifestyle.

Escape into imagination

A more constructive internalization of thoughts and feelings about being different is to escape into imagination. Some who have autism can develop a vivid and complex imaginary world as an alternative to reality. The imaginary world is safe from any predatory peers, perhaps featuring imaginary friends who are kind, understanding, and supportive. In this make-believe world the individual is respected and valued. Their experiences and outcomes are all under their control.

While escaping into imagination can be a very enjoyable experience, there are risks. For example, under conditions of extreme stress, social isolation and loneliness, the internal fantasy world may become an enjoyable "reality." But, the individual may be oblivious to his or her surroundings and to the reaction of other people, who may well misinterpret the person's state of mind.

The personality characteristics that indicate detachment from social relationships, such as not needing friendships or a close relationship, a preference for solitary activities, and an indifference to the praise or criticisms of others, can lead to a diagnosis of Schizoid Personality Disorder or be perceived as an early sign of schizophrenia. However, the ability to create alternative worlds can lead to a successful career as an author or playwright, and probably explains the great interest of some in fantasy, literature and films, alternative cultures, and periods of history, as well as avatar computer and Internet games.

Denial and arrogance

The alternative to internalizing thoughts of being different and defective is to externalize both the cause and the solution to these feelings. The individual develops a form of over-compensation by avidly denying he or she has any "defect," and claiming the "fault" is in other people. The individual may be desperate to conceal any social difficulties and not appear socially stupid. The individual finds comfort in feeling intellectually superior to others. This attitude can alienate peers. The individual tends to vehemently deny being different, rejecting programs to improve social understanding as "others have the problems, not me." Thus, there may be no motivation to change self-perception and no acknowledgment that there is value in accepting help and perceiving oneself more realistically in order to progress to the next degree.

The feelings of grandiosity, the perception of being special, and the need for admiration rather than correction, together with a sense of entitlement and arrogance, can lead to a secondary diagnosis of Narcissistic Personality Disorder.

Imitation

An intelligent and constructive compensatory mechanism is to observe, analyze, absorb, and imitate the characteristics and mannerisms of those who are socially successful. The strategy is to "wear a mask" to hide the real self, to "pretend to be normal," and to become the person other people would like you to be. It means becoming an expert mimic, "faking it 'til you make it," and creating a script for social situations based on observations of similar situations. This may lead to social acceptance, but the psychological and energy costs are excessive.

There can be intense performance anxiety prior to and during social interactions, and intense emotional and intellectual exhaustion afterward. There may be a great reluctance to reveal the true self, as there is a belief that person is defective and would be rejected. Imitation and the creation of a range of personas to achieve social integration and acceptance can lead to signs of episodic depression and a potential diagnosis of Dissociative Identity Disorder, previously known as Multiple Personality Disorder.

Other physical and mental health problems

In this third phase, the person consumes a great amount of energy to cope with being different and experiences considerable and continuously high levels of stress. We therefore expect the development of stress-related physical illnesses and a detrimental effect on the functioning of the immune system.

An instability in interpersonal relationships and self-image, volatile and difficult-to-manage anger, as well as fear of abandonment, identity disturbance, and suicidal ideation can all lead to a secondary diagnosis of Borderline Personality Disorder.

The person may also search for a "cure" and may be wondering if changing gender would resolve the interpersonal issues, or perhaps using alcohol and drugs to feel detached and safe from the aversive experiences of life.

Another coping mechanism is to become a recluse in one's bedroom, which effectively "dissolves" the main characteristic of autism, namely, the difficulty in social communication and social interaction. If there is no one to interact with, there is no social problem and no experience of rejection. The person can then be free to engage in an enjoyable special interest, which, because he or she is alone, does not annoy the family, who may otherwise insist on restricting access to the interest. Isolated in one's bedroom, there are no changes to routine and there is a stable and acceptable sensory environment. Thus, it is easy to understand why there may be a determination to maintain self-imposed isolation, and also why the person pursues the discovery of a functional "cure" and denies the need to progress to the fourth degree.

Fourth degree: self-identification

The goal of the fourth degree is to achieve an accurate sense of self, based on strengths rather than weaknesses, and not based on criticisms from peers or family members, or on trying to resolve past experiences. It is the deconstruction of the previous self-perception and the construction of a new concept of self.

To do this, the person will need a more objective self-reflection and a vocabulary of words and terms to describe the inner self. From my clinical experience, those who are on the autism spectrum have considerable difficulty with self-reflection and often have a limited vocabulary to describe and conceptualize inner thoughts and feelings. There can also be a limited vocabulary to describe different personality attributes and personality types.

However, self-expression and self-exploration can be achieved through the arts, such as poetry, music, writing fiction, drawing, painting, sculpture, and dance. To traverse this fourth degree of autism and achieve a paradigm shift in self-perception, it will be valuable to have a guide, perhaps a trusted family member, counselor, life coach, or psychologist, to help explore the inner self accurately and safely. The themes are "Who am I?" and "What are my qualities in terms of personality and abilities?," with the person completing questions such as "I am the sort of person who . . ."

This process can initially be resisted, but will subsequently become associated with a great sense of insight and relief. There will also be recognition of how the person is perceived by others and how he or she would like to be perceived. There can be a greater understanding of past experiences, a more realistic self-assessment, and an increased ability to explain the characteristics of autism accurately to others. There is an increasing knowledge of where to go to seek information, advice, and support and enjoyment in self-discovery and self-acceptance.

Many of those who have autism fail to achieve the fourth degree of autism, and thus we have much less knowledge regarding the remaining degrees of autism. However, the mature adults on the autism spectrum who have moved on with their lives are describing their journey, and psychologists are becoming increasingly aware of the many degrees of autism. Gradually, and together, we will be able to facilitate progression through all the degrees.

Fifth degree: considering all the options

True identity alignment requires recognition of the true self. This was always there but through psychological archaeology and self-reflection, the real self has now been identified. Not everyone who lives with autism will adjust easily to the new persona, but there is recent support from those who have autism, whom I describe as the wise mentors (Attwood, Evans, and Lesko, 2014).

During the fifth degree there may be closure with regard to past injustices and misinterpretations, and the recognition of a wide range of new options in life based on strengths and distinct qualities in personality and abilities. During this stage in the journey, the crisis of identity is resolved and the advantages of having autism recognized and embraced.

Sixth degree: crisis of identity/resolution to live with autism

I use the phrase "Be a first rate Aspie rather than a second rate neuro-typical" to explain the new identity. It is where the person becomes an expert on the real self and is able to explain simply and coherently those characteristics of autism that are confusing or abrasive to others. It is a time for the person to identify and be with those who are accepting, energizing, and enhancing, and to avoid the company of those who drain energy or create feelings of low self-esteem.

It is important for the person to identify circumstances that are nourishing, such as solitude, being in nature, and acquiring new skills and knowledge, and to recognize what depletes energy, such as trying to project a false persona and being with people who are "toxic" to mental health. This degree is about acknowledging which parts of the self to accept, which parts to change, and which parts cannot be changed.

Seventh degree: self-acceptance

It takes time to slowly absorb and integrate the changes and achieve self-acceptance. There will be new areas of fulfilment and enjoyment and the acquisition of abilities and experiences that had previously seemed so elusive. There is likely to be a new lifestyle, with consideration of the value of good nutrition and regular exercise. There may be a greater degree of assertiveness and self-reliance, and the possibility of new areas of study and employment.

Eighth degree: service to society

A sense of self in the eighth degree comes not only from conventional achievements based on social abilities and social networks, but on recognized and applauded achievements and service to society.

While we recognize that the brain of those who have autism is wired differently, it is not necessarily wired defectively, and can bestow remarkable and valuable talents in the sciences, arts, and humanities. Autism is a different way of perceiving and thinking and most of the major advances in science and information technology have been achieved by those who have many of the characteristics of the autism spectrum. Inner thoughts and feelings can be expressed not only in conversation, but in the arts, especially music, fine art, poetry, and prose. There are many with the traits of autism in the creative industries.

I have also recognized the strong sense of social justice and the compassion of those who have autism and their success in the caring professions, including psychology, psychiatry, nursing, and teaching. They are also valuable mentors to younger people who are on the autism spectrum.

Ninth degree: recognition, mastery and unity

The ultimate degree of autism is international recognition of the unique and innovative ability associated with autism that can enhance the lives of thousands of people, both neuro-typicals and those who have autism. There is the achievement of international recognition for specific skills, being a past master in terms of valued abilities, and having a legacy that will be appreciated for generations.

While only a few of those who live on the autism spectrum achieve this final degree of autism, they will change our perception of autism and often, how those with autism perceive themselves.

Reference

Attwood, T., Evans, C., & Lesko, A. (2014). *Been there, done that, try this! An Aspie guide to life on earth*. London: Jessica Kingsley Publishers.

2

A spectrum of neurodevelopment

Emily L. Casanova and Manuel F. Casanova

The dichotomous distinction between 'simple' and 'complex' diseases is completely artificial, and we argue instead for a model that considers a spectrum of diseases that are variably manifesting in each person.

(Lyon & O'Rawe, 2014, p. 2)

Though the pathology model is not popular amongst Neurodiversity proponents, we ask that you read the above quote with an open mind. Rather than thinking in terms of disease processes, instead broaden Lyon and O'Rawe's statement to include any observable characteristics (i.e., "phenotype") with which a person can present. The point that these authors are attempting to make is that no phenotype is the result of a single gene mutation. Even conditions that we scientists and doctors like to think of as one-gene or Mendelian can be quite variable in the symptoms they present and are subject to an individual's genetic background and environment. True, there may be a core set of traits that all or most people with the condition have, but secondary features and even the severity of the primary features themselves fluctuate from person to person.

For this very reason, autism is referred to as a "spectrum" because it's a multifaceted condition that manifests in different ways from person to person. Not only is there a range of severity in the primary features, but there are also different secondary conditions that can co-occur with autism, a term known as "comorbidity." For instance, some individuals may be plagued by extreme hypersensitivities due to sensory processing disorder (SPD), others may have specific learning disabilities (LD) that can make school or work difficult without accommodations, and others still may have Tourette's syndrome, attention deficit hyperactivity disorder (ADHD), bipolar disorder, obsessive-compulsive disorder (OCD), anxiety disorders, or even intellectual disability (mental retardation). These are just a few of the comorbid conditions that can complicate the autism picture, sometimes making it a challenge for accurate diagnosis. This may be a particular challenge when diagnosing high-functioning adults whose symptom expressions can be masked due to learned adaptation.

Why do so many conditions so frequently occur together? The answer is that they probably don't. Recent research is beginning to suggest that many neurodevelopmental conditions share similar causes even though behaviorally they may appear quite different, which would explain why they overlap so frequently. It would also explain why, when researchers study the genetics of these different conditions, they tend to see some of the same genes indicated over and over again. In stark contrast, however, there appears to be a huge range of gene mutations that can affect autism risk, suggesting that many genotypes (i.e., genetic backgrounds) can funnel into a similar phenotype.

In this chapter, we're going to address why there may be so much comorbidity among different neurodevelopmental conditions and how that provides a challenge to diagnosticians and patients seeking a diagnosis. To do this, we'll also be pulling from examples in the fields of genetics and neuroscience to try to understand whether these conditions have more in common than meets the eye.

What does genetics tell us?

Are 'diabetes', 'schizophrenia' or 'coronary artery disease' any more specific than 'mental retardation' as diagnoses? If two patients had different underlying causes, would we have any way to know this on the basis of their symptom profiles? Is it not possible, even likely, that as with blindness or mental retardation, many different insults could give rise to a similar end-state? This is especially likely if our descriptors are crude. For psychiatric disorders, for example, there is no definitive biomarker, brain scan or blood test that can aid in clinical diagnosis. These disorders are defined on the basis of surface criteria: the patient's behavior and reports of their subjective experience. The diagnostic categories are constantly being debated and the borders between them redefined. Many patients' diagnoses are fluid over time and two patients can have the same diagnosis without sharing a single symptom in common.

(Mitchell, 2012, p. 237)

Examples of single mutations causing disorders such as autism, schizophrenia, diabetes, epilepsy and many other common diseases have long been known. While these could be identified in only a small proportion of cases, they could, however, be disregarded as exceptions to the generality of the disease: they did not cause 'real schizophrenia' or 'real autism'. But what if there is no such thing? What if all cases are due to some rare mutation?

(Mitchell, 2012, p. 237)

For research and clinical purposes, autism spectrum conditions (ASC) are divided into two main categories: idiopathic and genetic. "Idiopathic" means that the causes for these types of autism are unknown. Meanwhile, "genetic" indicates that scientists have identified some gene variant or larger chromosomal disruption that is strongly linked to the presence of autism symptoms. Most of the genetic forms of autism are also "syndromic," named so because they tend to have other characteristics that occur alongside the autism, such as malformations of the face or hands and feet, and dysfunction in other organ systems like the heart or kidneys. While genetic forms of autism make up only a minority of cases in the larger autistic population, they still account for a significant minority, with current estimations ranging from 15–20% of the autism spectrum (Stein et al., 2013).

Though it's infrequently acknowledged, autism can also include a third category, called "teratogenic." A teratogen is an agent that affects development of the embryo or fetus. This can come in the form of a medication, for example, that the mother takes during pregnancy, or even maternal infections that can affect development.

While the range of agents we know for certain that affect autism risk are few, we do know, for instance, that prenatal exposure to the anti-epileptic Depakote (Valproate) can significantly increase risk for autism by about 10-fold (Moore et al., 2000). The drug Thalidomide, which was used in Europe during the mid-20th century to treat morning sickness, is also linked with approximately 4-fold increased autism risk (Strömland et al., 1994).

In addition, we know that maternal rubella infection significantly increases autism incidence in fetuses exposed (Chess, 1971). And more recently, there has been research indicating that gestational diabetes and similar maternal metabolic syndromes might affect risk, though further work into causal mechanisms is still needed (Krakowiak et al., 2012).

As a disclaimer, when we use the term "cause" as in "a gene mutation causes a condition," this is a generalization and the truth of the science is not so simple. In actuality, a gene mutation may heavily factor into the development of a particular condition, but by no means is it the sole variable.

This is undoubtedly why there is so much symptom variability even within a single Mendelian condition. For example, not all individuals with mutations in the handful of genes that lead to Fragile X Syndrome develop autism, although a large minority do (Rogers et al., 2001). We're not exactly sure why that is but it likely has to do not only with minor variations between different mutations themselves, but also with the genetic background and environment of each individual. In other words, *variety results from the context within which a variable effects change.* So please take the term "cause" with a grain of salt in this chapter as it's used solely for the sake of simplicity rather than accuracy.

What do we know about the genetics of autism? For one, we know that several thousand different genes have been implicated in the condition. Most of these share only modest and potentially dubious links with autism, but a couple hundred in particular seem to have moderate-to-strong associations, making them good candidates for further study. A couple hundred risk genes probably sounds like a lot for a condition to which we apply a single label, "The Autism Spectrum," and it is. But this is why it's referred to as a "complex condition," in contrast to a rare disorder that tends to have one or maybe a few genes that cause it (Gilissen et al., 2011).

When we talk about "autism," we're not actually talking about a single condition but a large group of conditions that share overlapping core symptoms. This is probably one of the biggest reasons why the phrase "When you've met one person with autism, you've only met one person with autism" rings so true.

Because the genetic background of autism is so complex and heterogeneous, some scientists believe therefore that the only things autistic people have in common lie at the behavioral level. And it is indeed true that when one studies the range of functions of different genes implicated in the condition, it's a challenge to find common ground.

However, other scientists such as ourselves believe that autistic people have more than just behaviors in common but that these behaviors are reflective of a core neurophysiology. By "neurophysiology" we refer to the function of the brain. If this is true, it implies that many different gene mutations and perhaps even environmental exposures, such as infection, can lead to similar neurodevelopmental effects and ultimately to overlapping autistic traits. These different causes converge or are funneled into a similar phenotype. But is that even possible?

Recent research suggests that it's definitely possible. Our laboratory in particular has been entranced by the idea that different gene mutations can lead to a common outcome. To study this idea, we gathered together a list of a couple hundred autism-risk genes with modest-to-strong association with the condition and investigated whether overexpression or loss-of-function mutations in these genes affected neuronal development and in what ways that occurred (Casanova & Casanova, 2014).

To give some background into how the brain develops, initially the embryonic nervous system produces neural stem cells. These stem cells expand their numbers for a certain period of time by a process called "symmetric division." The term "symmetric" indicates that when a neural stem cell divides, it produces two identical neural stem cells, effectively increasing the size of the stem cell pool. Eventually, some of these stem cells start switching to "asymmetric division" in which one neural stem cell and one newborn neuron (neuroblast) are produced. This process is also known as "neurogenesis," the birth of new neurons. There are variations on this basic theme, but this is the overall premise.

The newborn neuron or neuroblast starts to mature. Often this involves an intermediate stage of travel or migration to its final location. Once it's managed to find its final resting place, the neuron starts to sprout extensions known as "neurites." First comes the neurite that will eventually become the "axon," which is used to send signals to other neurons (the output). Next come the neurites that will develop into "dendrites," which are the branches that receive incoming signals from other neurons (the input). Once the neurites have matured, they start to sprout "synapses," which are small protrusions that serve as communicative junctions between nerve cells. At this point, we consider this neuron a mature adult cell. Usually the term used in the study of cell biology to indicate this maturity is "fully differentiated."

What we have found through studying the genetics of autism is that neurons may fail to mature properly, leading to differences in how they integrate into and communicate with the larger network of cells. This matches well with postmortem examinations of the brains of autistic people in which particular types of malformations are extremely common, particularly within the cerebral cortex (see Casanova & Casanova, 2014, for review). The majority of the genes that we studied affect neurogenesis and maturation of the newborn neuron, especially during stages preceding its migration. Many of these same genes also affect later stages of neuronal maturation, during the time of neurite extension and synapse development. These findings indicate that many stages of neuronal development are probably affected in autism.

But why is proper maturation so important for a neuron? In an extremely complex organ such as the brain, a cell's identity is everything. A cell's identity, its molecular makeup, is crucial in determining how it will connect and interact with the other cells around it. If it fails to develop properly, it may also fail to make proper connections, changing how the brain communicates with itself. An excellent example relevant to autism lies with the neurotransmitter, gamma-aminobutyric acid (GABA).

Neurotransmitters are small chemicals that neurons send to one another in order to communicate information, and GABA is the primary inhibitory neurotransmitter in the postnatal brain. However, prenatally, it serves as an excitatory neurotransmitter, helping to orchestrate the proliferation of cells, their migrations, and ultimately how they branch and connect with one another.

There are a variety of markers that indicate whether GABA is behaving in an excitatory or inhibitory fashion in the brain. Interestingly, abnormal expression of some of these markers has been implicated in autism, epilepsy, schizophrenia, and bipolar, suggesting that GABA may be acting in an excitatory manner in these conditions (Lemonnier et al., 2012; Dzhala et al., 2005; Hyde et al., 2011; Guidotti et al., 2000). While we won't bore you with the specific markers used to investigate these features in autism and the like, we will take a moment to explain in simple terms how a single neurotransmitter, GABA, can exhibit such divergent functions.

The effects of GABA are mitigated by negatively charged chloride particles. When the neurotransmitter, GABA, docks on the GABA receptor located on the outside of the cell it causes a chloride channel to open. When this occurs, chloride ions are allowed to flow through the channel. The primary difference between a mature and immature neuron in this respect is whether the chloride ions flow *into* or *out of* the cell. You see, in a mature neuron, there are more chloride ions outside the cell. Therefore, when the channel opens they rush toward the site of lowest concentration, which in this case lies within the neuron.

This subsequently causes a drop in charge within the neuron because these ions are negatively charged. Neurons have a minimum positive threshold they must acquire in order to fire and communicate with other cells. Thus, as you can imagine, a drop in positive charge leads to the suppression of neural firing. And this is how GABA functions as an inhibitory neurotransmitter in mature neurons.

However, in immature neurons, more chloride resides within the cell. And therefore when a chloride channel opens, the ions rush outside, causing an immediate rise in positive charge within the cell. If the charge rises high enough to reach its threshold, the neuron will fire. And this is how a single neurotransmitter, GABA, fulfills two extremely different functions (Figure 2.1).

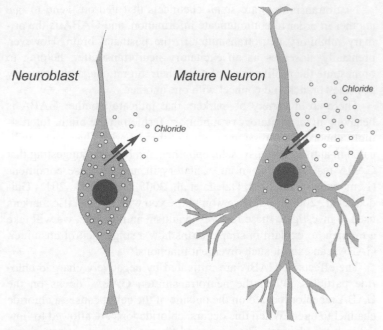

Neuroblast   *Mature Neuron*

Chloride

Chloride

Figure 2.1

The drug Bumetanide helps to decrease internal concentrations of chloride within the cell, improving the inhibitory capacity of GABA. Interestingly, its use has met with success in both autism and epilepsy (Lemonnier et al., 2012; Dzhala et al., 2005). In addition, early studies suggest that it has had positive effects in an animal model of anxiety, therefore it not only holds promise as an intervention for anxiety sufferers, but also it indicates that abnormal chloride concentrations may be integral in anxiety formation both in autism and in the general population (Krystal et al., 2012). In general, this wealth of evidence arising from both the fields of genetics and cellular biology indicate that neuronal maturation is disturbed in autism and related conditions.

Similar disturbance, different networks?

Though it used to be considered an anxiety disorder, under the new *Diagnostic and Statistical Manual of Mental Disorders 5 (DSM-5)*, OCD and its related conditions now head their own chapter. As may be all too familiar to most readers, obsessive-compulsive–like behaviors are part and parcel of the autism diagnosis, though the quality may vary somewhat in terms of the complexity of routines and rituals compared to typical OCD (Zandt et al., 2007).

Conversely, research also suggests that a significant minority (20%) of those with OCD exhibit autistic traits, once again suggesting overlap in causality (Bejerot et al., 2001). Like OCD, Tourette's syndrome frequently overlaps with autism, with 35% of those with Tourette's fulfilling criteria for ASC (CDC, 2014). Interestingly, more than one third of those with Tourette's also have OCD (CDC, 2014). In addition, according to the CDC, 63% have comorbid ADHD, 49% have anxiety problems, 47% have a LD, 28% are developmentally delayed, and 12% have intellectual disability.

Aside from molecular overlap, these comorbid conditions may display overlap in the structures most responsible for the core symptoms. As background, the cerebral cortex communicates with a set of nuclei in the brain known as the basal ganglia.

While it's not particularly important to understand where these nuclei are located and the subtleties of their various functions, it is important to know that the basal ganglia behave somewhat like a funnel, capable of either amplifying or suppressing information sent to them from the cortex.

Once this occurs, the information is routed back to the cerebral cortex through the thalamus. There are a number of large circuits that run from different portions of the cortex to different portions of the basal ganglia and thalamic nuclei, though the best-studied circuit is the motor circuit. You may already be somewhat familiar with what dysfunction in this circuit can do: for instance, disturbances to the motor circuit lead to the symptoms of rigidity and tremor in Parkinson's disease (Obeso et al., 2000). Parkinsonian-like tremor can also be seen both in drug-naïve and medicated schizophrenics, although medication in the latter group tends to exacerbate the motor symptoms (Caligiuri et al., 1993) (Figure 2.2).

Symptoms of both OCD and Tourette's are rooted in these cortex/basal ganglia circuits, otherwise known as "cortico-subcortical circuits." While the specific circuits affected in each condition vary somewhat, both appear to be the result of dysfunctional loops that fail to suppress unwanted information, leading to repetitive thoughts, compulsions, and tics (DeLong & Wichmann, 2007). Interestingly, functional and volumetric differences have been noted in the basal

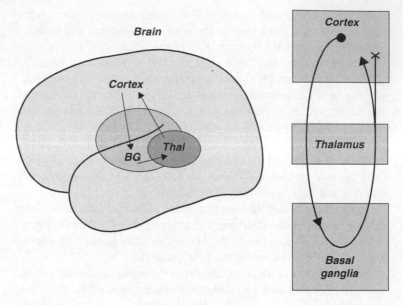

Figure 2.2

ganglia in autism as well, suggesting a reason for both the overlap in symptomology and comorbidity (Turner et al., 2006; Estes et al., 2011).

According to Simonoff et al. (2008), approximately 28% of autistic children will also fulfill full criteria for ADHD, and most in fact present with symptoms of executive dysfunction (Hughes et al., 1994). In addition, twin studies indicate that autism and ADHD are strongly correlated in the general population, suggesting common inherited influences (Ronald et al., 2008).

In 1990, it was proposed by Posner and Peterson that attention is divided into three primary networks (reviewed in Peterson & Posner, 2012). These networks include the *Alerting Network*, which tells the brain when a new signal has arisen, the *Orienting Network*, which tells the brain where that signal is coming from, and the *Executive Control Network*, which is subsequently subdivided into two additional networks, both of which are involved in focal attention.

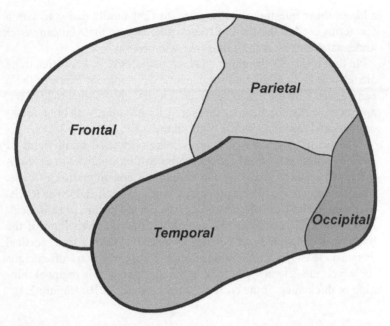

Figure 2.3

One of these subnetworks, the cingulo-opercular control system, aids in sustained attention during a task, meanwhile, the frontoparietal system is involved in task initiation and successful task switching, e.g., multitasking (Dosenbach et al., 2008). Lesion studies, resulting in the development of ADHD following childhood stroke, reveal that the location of damage typically involves the frontal lobes, suggesting their involvement in idiopathic ADHD as well (Max et al., 2005) (Figure 2.3).

In particular, it suggests that the core symptoms of ADHD involve dysfunction in *Executive Control*. Interestingly, connectivity within the *Executive Control* subnetwork, the frontoparietal system, also appears to be significantly affected in OCD, suggesting a relationship between obsessions/compulsions and the OCDer's difficulty in disengaging from particular thoughts and compulsive tasks (Stern et al., 2012).

How do all of these findings fit together? Do they suggest, as we have posited in some of our own work, that the maturation of neurons is disturbed in these different but overlapping neurodevelopmental conditions, leading to their similarities and comorbidities? To further address these questions, we're going to first familiarize you with a few terms used in the field of Neuropathology, so that you can better understand the research findings we will present.

In the field of Developmental Neuropathology, we know that there are tell-tale signs to disruptions in neural development. Some of these can be seen with the naked eye if the scientist knows what to look for, and meanwhile others can be measured, for instance, with brain imaging and analyzed via specific algorithms.

The word "dysplasia" is a term commonly used in all fields of Pathology and, at its most general, refers to abnormalities in development, particularly involving the maturation and migration of cells. This can refer to dysplastic processes both at the cell and tissue levels. Many times these dysplasias are not tissue-wide but are instead focalized. When this occurs in the cerebral cortex or cerebellum of the brain, it is called a "focal cortical dysplasia." When a focal cortical dysplasia (FCD) occurs in the cerebral cortex, there are often signs for which the scientist can look. An important sign is regional thinning or thickening of the cortex (Blümcke et al., 2010) (Figure 2.4).

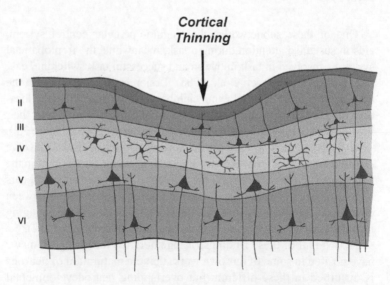

Figure 2.4

Interestingly, focal differences in cortical thickness, i.e., dysplasia, have been noted in autism, ADHD, OCD, major depression, bipolar, Tourette's, schizophrenia, epilepsy, and various forms of intellectual disability (Jiao et al., 2010; Makris et al., 2007; Fallucca et al., 2011; Lyoo et al., 2006; Narr et al., 2005; Sowell et al., 2008; McDonald et al., 2008; Bearden et al., 2007). However, each condition seems to exhibit variations in the regions affected or the extent of the effects. This suggests that, given the hereditary overlap and high rates of comorbidity between them, the primary difference between these conditions isn't necessarily one of quality but in the specific regions affected.

In other words, disturbances to neuronal maturation may predispose toward a variety of interrelated neurodevelopmental conditions yet vary by person according to the structures and regions most severely affected. In the next section we'll address how this spectrum of neurodevelopment can lead to diagnostic difficulties, particularly when dealing with people who have complicated diagnostic profiles or whose adaptive abilities overshadow ongoing developmental challenges.

Muddying the diagnostic waters

For adults who are high functioning or have complex symptom profiles (or both), achieving an accurate and useful diagnosis can often be difficult. One hurdle is that most diagnosticians are more familiar with autism presentation in childhood as opposed to adulthood. Thus, autistic people may instead receive a host of various comorbid diagnoses which, while perhaps technically accurate, don't capture the full symptom picture nor provide for understanding of subtler deficits that may be core to autism but not conditions like ADHD, OCD, or learning disability. Therefore, higher-functioning adults may find themselves "doctor shopping" until they reach someone who is familiar with the nuanced and complex symptom profiles sometimes present in adulthood.

Other difficulties may also arise when diagnosing adult high-functioning females, who may present with comparatively subtler social deficits than males yet still suffer impairment from symptoms related to autism. This is illustrated well in a study by Lai et al. (2011)

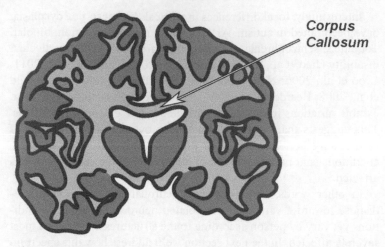

Figure 2.5

in which high-functioning adult autistic females appeared to have fewer socio-communication challenges than their male counterparts, although conversely the women also exhibited more symptoms of sensory processing disorder. Interestingly, genetics research suggests that the female sex plays a protective role in terms of autism severity.

A recent publication by Jacquemont et al. (2014) reported that females often require additional genetic burden in order for the condition to manifest at a similar severity as seen in males. In support of this, another study found that siblings of autistic females were usually more severely affected than siblings of autistic males, indicating that the hereditary load in families of autistic females is comparatively heavier (Robinson et al., 2013). This gender difference in autism susceptibility is referred to as the "Female Protective Model" and not only resonates with the diagnostic gender disparity seen in autism but may also explain the differences in socio-communicative severity in high-functioning females versus males.

One potential explanation for differences in socio-communicative impairment between male and female autistics may be partly due to gender dimorphism of the human brain. Females, on average, tend to have smaller brain volumes than men, a finding that agrees with differences in overall body size. While it's uncertain whether the effect is one solely of brain size or is complicated by gender-specific influences, it seems apparent that smaller brains tend to have larger corpus callosa for their sizes (Jäncke et al., 1997). The corpus callosum is the large tract of fibers that connects the two cerebral hemispheres, allowing them to communicate.

If one looks at the spectrum of human brain volumes, one will find that as the size of the brain increases there are also modest increases in the size of the corpus callosum. However, according to a recent study by Hänggi et al. (2014), this effect is more exaggerated in the female brain as compared to males. While short-range tracts allow the brain to compartmentalize and specialize, long-range tracts such as the corpus callosum allow it to integrate a broad range of disparate information. Socialization and communication are two tasks that require extensive cognitive coordination.

Interestingly, the size of the corpus callosum in autism is comparatively reduced, potentially explaining some of the socio-communicative deficits (Casanova et al., 2009). If, however, female autistics, like their typical counterparts, have a greater level of interconnectivity than male autistics, it may well explain why their deficits in socio-communication are less severe yet they may match their male counterparts in the repetitive/restricted behaviors domain. It may also explain why high-functioning women are diagnostically overlooked (Attwood, 2012) (Figure 2.5).

The comorbid complexity of autism is indeed extensive. A recent report presented at an Interagency Autism Coordinating Committee workshop by Lisa Croen (2014) from the Kaiser Permanente Division of Research stated that anxiety, depression, ADHD, bipolar, psychotic disorders, and OCD were all significantly elevated in adults with autism versus controls. ADHD, for instance, was over 5 times as common in autistic adults than their control counterparts; meanwhile, bipolar was close to 6 times as likely, OCD a remarkable 14.6 times as likely, and psychotic disorders an astounding 22 times as common in autism than in controls.

In another study on children and young adolescents with autism, it was found that 70% had at least one comorbid neurodevelopmental condition, meanwhile 41% had two or more (Simonoff et al., 2008). These included social anxiety, ADHD, and oppositional defiant disorder (ODD).

Of those who had a diagnosis of autism and ADHD, 84% had a third neurodevelopmental diagnosis. Another study by Leyfer et al. (2006) found that in children with autism, 44% had at least one specific phobia (e.g., fear of needles), 37% met criteria for OCD, 31% for ADHD, and 10% had had at least one major depressive episode. In another study by van Steensel et al. (2013), they found that while rates of comorbid disorders didn't significantly differ between children with autism and children with ADHD, those with autism had higher rates of anxiety disorders.

In summary, all of these studies and the many more which have been performed on autism comorbidities paint a consistent yet complicated picture. As you might imagine, comorbid conditions can easily mask the autism when the latter is less severe or atypical in presentation, particularly if the individual has managed to adapt well enough to hide underlying difficulties.

The broader neurodevelopmental spectrum

There is a broad agreement that genetic influences are central in the development of idiopathic autism. Whether relatives manifest genetically milder phenotypes, and if so how these relate to autism proper, has proved a more contentious issue. A review of the relevant studies indicates that relatives are sometimes affected by difficulties that appear conceptually related to autistic behaviors. These range in severity from pervasive developmental disorders to abnormalities in only one area of functioning, and possibly extend to related personality traits.

(Bailey et al., 1998, p. 369)

Many readers are probably somewhat familiar with the concept of a Broader Autism Phenotype (BAP), a term which refers to the portion of the broader autism spectrum whose traits are sub-threshold for official diagnosis. Even as early as the 1940s, Leo Kanner and Hans Asperger both individually noted milder autistic-like manifestations in parents of the children they were studying (Sucksmith et al., 2011).

Later, Folstein and Rutter (1977) studied autism concordance among identical and fraternal twins, reporting that 82% of identical twins shared a broader range of "cognitive abnormalities," a finding which some scientists believe hinted at the existence of BAP (Sucksmith et al., 2011). By 1998, Bailey et al. proposed the existence of BAP and researchers have since tried to study it as its own entity.

As may be of little surprise, many of the common comorbid neu-rodevelopmental conditions exhibit subclinical manifestations as well, a sort of Broader Neurodevelopmental Spectrum (BNS). Those broader phenotypes that have been better studied include ADHD, OCD, schizophrenia, bipolar, depression, and anxiety (Kóbor et al., 2012; Black & Gaffney, 2008; Hain et al., 1995; Kwapil et al., 2011; Martin et al., 1996; Andrea et al., 2004). Therefore, not only do these different conditions strongly overlap, they are each spectrums unto themselves, blending into the general population.

Medicine and science have the tendency to go through cycles of lumping and splitting concepts. Until recently, conditions such as autism, ADHD, and OCD were split according to variations in symptomology and their frequent comorbidities were treated as something more or less coincidental. More recently, however, clinicians and scientists have begun lumping the spectrum of common comorbid neurodevelopmental conditions together. As Christopher Gillberg writes,

> There is good evidence that ASD and ADHD can be separate and recognizable "disorders", but, equally, there is mounting evidence that they often overlap, constitute amalgams of problems, and that in some families they separate together and probably represent different aspects of the same underlying disorder.
>
> (Gillberg, 2010, p. 1544)

The same can be said of other neurodevelopmental conditions and, for this reason, Gillberg has proposed that this group of inter-related phenotypes be viewed under a single umbrella term known as E.S.S.E.N.C.E., which stands for Early Symptomatic Syndromes Eliciting Neurodevelopmental Clinical Examinations and includes all of the conditions discussed in this chapter. The purpose of this acronym, according to Gillberg, is to highlight the fact that in the clinic, comorbidities are the rule rather than the exception.

The fact that these conditions exhibit spectrums of severity that blend into normality and strongly overlap one another leads to extensive variation in the human population and diagnostic headaches for clinician and patient alike. When we attempt to place people into well-defined symptomological boxes, invariably some individuals will fail to fit. At that point, it's important for the clinician to have a nuanced understanding of how these different conditions relate to one another and how problem symptoms may be masked or overlooked. In order to not overlook such difficulties, it is highly recommended that any individual presenting with E.S.S.E.N.C.E.–like symptoms be given a full diagnostic workup covering the range of common comorbid neurodevelopmental conditions.

References

Andrea, H., Bülltmann, U., Beurskens, A. J., Swaen, G. M., van Schayck, C. P., & Kant, I. J. (2004). Anxiety and depression in the working population using the HAD scale – Psychometrics, prevalence and relationships with psychosocial work characteristics. *Social Psychiatry and Psychiatric Epidemiology, 39*, 637–646.

Attwood, T. (2012). Girls with Asperger's syndrome: Early diagnosis is critical. *Autism Asperger's Digest.* Retrieved from http://autism-digest.com/girls-with-a/

Bailey, A., Palferman, S., Heavey, L., & Le Couteur, A. (1998). Autism: The phenotype in relatives. *Journal of Autism and Developmental Disorders, 28*, 369–392.

Bearden, C. E., van Erp, T. G., Dutton, R. A., Tran, H., Zimmerman, L., Sun, D., et al. (2007). Mapping cortical thickness in children with 22q11.2 deletions. *Cerebral Cortex, 17*, 1889–1898.

Bejerot, S., Nylander, L., & Lindström, E. (2001). Autistic traits in obsessive-compulsive disorder. *Nordic Journal of Psychiatry, 55*, 169–176.

Black, D. W., & Gaffney, G. R. (2008). Subclinical obsessive-compulsive disorder in children and adolescents: Additional results from a "high-risk" study. *CNS Spectrums, 13*, 54–61.

Blümcke, I., Thom, M., Aronica, E., Armstrong, D. D., Vinters, H. V., Palmini, A., et al. (2010). The clinicopathologic spectrum of focal cortical dysplasia: A consensus classification proposed by an hoc Task Force of the ILAE Diagnostic Methods Commission. *Epilepsia, 52*, 158–174.

Caligiuri, M. P., Lohr, J. B., & Jeste, D. V. (1993). Parkinsonism in neuroleptic-naïve schizophrenic patients. *The American Journal of Psychiatry, 150*, 1343–1348.

Casanova, E. L., & Casanova, M. F. (2014). Genetics studies indicate that neural induction and early neuronal maturation are disturbed in autism. *Frontiers in Cellular Neuroscience*, doi:10.3389/fncel.2014.00397

Casanova, M. F., El-Baz, A., Mott, M., Mannheim, G., Hassan, H., Fahmi, R., et al. (2009). Reduced gyral window and corpus callosum size in autism: Possible macroscopic correlates of a minicolumnopathy. *Journal of Autism and Developmental Disorders, 39*, 751–764.

Centers for Disease Control (CDC). (2014). *Tourette syndrome (TS): Data & statistics*. Retrieved from http://www.cdc.gov/ncbddd/tourette/data.html

Chess, S. (1971). Autism in children with congenital rubella. *Journal of Autism and Childhood Schizophrenia, 1*, 33–47.

Croen, L. (2014). Psychiatric and medical conditions among adults with ASD. *IACC Workshop on Under-recognized Co-occurring Conditions in ASD*. September 23.

DeLong, M. R., & Wichmann, T. (2007). Circuits and circuit disorders of the basal ganglia. *Archives of Neurology, 64*, 20–24.

Dosenbach, N. U. F., Fair, D. A., Cohen, A. L., Schlaggar, B. L., & Petersen, S. E. (2008). A dual-networks architecture of top-down control. *Trends in Cognitive Sciences, 12*, 99–105.

Dzhala, V. I., Talos, D. M., Sdrulla, D. A., Brumback, A. C., Mathews, G. C., Benke, T. A., et al. (2005). NKCC1 transporter facilitates seizures in the developing brain. *Nature Medicine, 11*, 1205–1213.

Estes, A., Shaw, D. W., Sparks, B. F., Friedman, S., Giedd, J. N., Dawson, G., et al. (2011). Basal ganglia morphometry and repetitive behavior in young children with autism spectrum disorder. *Autism Research, 4*, 212–220.

Fallucca, E., MacMaster, F. P., Haddad, J., Easter, P., Dick, R., May, G., et al. (2011). Distinguishing between major depressive disorder and obsessive-compulsive disorder in children by measuring regional cortical thickness. *Archives of General Psychiatry, 68*, 527–533.

Folstein, S., & Rutter, M. (1977). Infantile autism: A genetic study of 21 twin pairs. *Journal of Child Psychology and Psychiatry, 18*, 297–321.

Gilissen, C., Hoischen, A., Brunner, H. G., & Veltman, J. A. (2011). Unlocking Mendelian disease using exome sequencing. *Genome Biology, 12*, 228.

Gillberg, C. (2010). The ESSENCE in child psychiatry: Early Symptomatic Syndromes Eliciting Neurodevelopmental Clinical Examinations. *Research in Developmental Disabilities, 31*, 1543–1551.

Guidotti, A., Auta, J., Davis, J.M., Di-Giorgi-Gerevini, V., Dwivedi, Y., Grayson, D.R., et al. (2000). Decrease in reelin and glutamic acid decarboxylase67 (GAD67) expression in schizophrenia and bipolar disorder: A postmortem brain study. *Archives of General Psychiatry, 57*, 1061–1069.

Hain, C., Maier, W., Hoeschst-Janneck, S., & Franke, P. (1995). Subclinical thought disorder in first-degree relatives of schizophrenic patients. Results from a matched-pairs study with the Thought Disorder Index. *Acta Psychiatrica Scandinavia, 92*, 305–309.

Hänggi, J., Fövenyi, L., Liem, F., Meyer, M., & Jäncke, L. (2014). The hypothesis of neuronal interconnectivity as a function of brain size – A general organization principle of the human connectome. *Frontiers in Human Neuroscience, 8*, 915.

Hughes, C., Russell, J., & Robbins, T.W. (1994). Evidence for executive dysfunction in autism. *Neuropsychologia, 32*, 477–492.

Hyde, T.M., Lipska, B.K., Ali, T., Mathew, S.V., Law, A.J., Metitiri, O.E., et al. (2011). Expression of GABA signaling molecules KCC2, NKCC1, and GAD1 in cortical development and schizophrenia. *Journal of Neuroscience, 31*, 11088–11095.

Jacquemont, S., Coe, B.P., Hersch, M., Duyzend, M.H., Krumm, N., Bergmann, S., et al. (2014). A higher mutational burden in females supports a "female protective model" in neurodevelopmental disorders. *American Journal of Human Genetics, 94*, 415–425.

Jäncke, L., Staiger, J.F., Schlaug, G., Huang, Y., & Steinmetz, H. (1997). The relationship between corpus callosum size and forebrain volume. *Cerebral Cortex, 7*, 48–56.

Jiao, Y., Chen, R., Ke, X., Chu, K., Lu, Z., & Herskovits, E.H. (2010). Predictive models of autism spectrum disorder based on brain regional cortical thickness. *Neuroimage, 50*, 589–599.

Kóbor, A., Takács, Á., Urbán, R., & Csépe, V. (2012). The latent classes of subclinical ADHD symptoms: Convergences of multiple informant reports. *Research in Developmental Disabilities, 33*, 1677–1689.

Krakowiak, P., Walker, C.K., Bremer, A.A., Baker, A.S., Ozonoff, S., Hansen, R.L., et al. (2012). Maternal metabolic conditions and risk for autism and other neurodevelopmental disorders. *Pediatrics, 129,* e1121–e1128.

Krystal, A. D., Sutherland, J., and Hochman, D. W. (2012). Loop diuretics have anxiolytic effects in rat models of conditioned anxiety. *PLoS One, 7,* e35417.

Kwapil, T. R., Barrantes-Vidal, N., Armistead, M. S., Hope, G. A., Brown, L. H., Silvia, P. J., et al. (2011). The expression of bipolar spectrum psychopathology in daily life. *Journal of Affective Disorders, 130,* 166–170.

Lai, M. C., Lombardo, M. V., Pasco, G., Ruigrok, A. N., Wheelwright, S. J., Sadek, S. A., et al. (2011). A behavioral comparison of male and female adults with high functioning autism spectrum conditions. *PLoS One, 6,* e20835.

Lemonnier, E., Degrez, C., Phelep, M., Tyzio, R., Josse, F., Grandgeorge, M., et al. (2012). A randomised controlled trial of bumetanide in the treatment of autism children. *Translational Psychiatry, 2,* e202.

Leyfer, O. T., Folstein, S. E., Bacalman, S., Davis, N. O., Dinh, E., Morgan, J., et al. (2006). Comorbid psychiatric disorders in children with autism: Interview development and rates of disorders. *Journal of Autism and Developmental Disorders, 36,* 849–861.

Lyon, G. J., & O'Rawe, J. (2014). Human genetics and clinical aspects of neurodevelopmental disorders. *bioRXiv beta,* p. 2. doi:http://dx.doi.org/10.1101/000687

Lyoo, I. K., Sung, Y. H., Dager, S. R., Friedman, S. D., Lee, J. Y., Kim, S. J., et al. (2006). Regional cerebral cortical thinning in bipolar disorder. *Bipolar Disorders, 8,* 65–74.

Makris, N., Biederman, J., Valera, E. M., Bush, G., Kaiser, J., Kennedy, D. N., et al. (2007). Cortical thinning of the attention and executive function networks in adults with attention-deficit/hyperactivity disorder. *Cerebral Cortex, 17,* 1364–1375.

Martin, J. K., Blum, T. C., Beach, S. R., & Roman, P. M. (1996). Subclinical depression and performance at work. *Social Psychiatry and Psychiatric Epidemiology, 31,* 3–9.

Max, J. E., Manes, F. F., Robertson, B. A., Mathews, K., Fox, P. T., & Lancaster, J. (2005). Prefrontal and executive attention network lesions and the development of attention-deficit/hyperactivity symptomatology. *Journal of the American Academy of Child and Adolescent Psychiatry, 44,* 443–450.

McDonald, C. R., Hagler, D. J., Jr., Admadi, M. E., Tecoma, E., Iragui, V., Gharapetian, L., et al. (2008). Regional neocortical thinning in mesial temporal lobe epilepsy. *Epilepsia, 49*, 794–803.

Mitchell, K. J. (2012). What is complex about complex disorders? *Genome Biology, 13*, 237.

Moore, S. J., Turnpenny, P., Quinn, A., Glover, S., Lloyd, D. J., Montgomery, T., et al. (2000). A clinical study of 57 children with fetal anticonvulsant syndromes. *Journal of Medical Genetics, 37*, 489–497.

Narr, K. L., Toga, A. W., Szeszko, P., Thompson, P. M., Woods, R. P., Robinson, D., et al. (2005). Cortical thinning in cingulate and occipital cortices in first episode schizophrenia. *Biological Psychiatry, 58*, 32–40.

Obeso, J. A., Rodriguez-Oroz, M. C., Rodriguez, M., Lanciego, J. L., Artieda, J., Gonzalo, N., et al. (2000). Pathophysiology of the basal ganglia in Parkinson's disease. *Trends in Neurosciences, 23*, S8–S19.

Peterson, S. E., & Posner, M. I. (2012). The attention system of the human brain: 20 years after. *Annual Review of Neuroscience, 35*, 73.

Robinson, E. B., Lichtenstein, P., Anckarsäter, H., Happé, F., & Ronald, A. (2013). Examining and interpreting the female protective effect against autistic behavior. *Proceedings of the National Academy of Sciences, USA, 110*, 5258–5262.

Rogers, S. J., Wehner, D. E., & Hagerman, R. (2001). The behavioral phenotype in fragile X: Symptoms of autism in very young children with fragile X syndrome, idiopathic autism, and other developmental disorders. *Journal of Developmental and Behavioral Pediatrics, 22*, 409–417.

Ronald, A., Simonoff, E., Kuntsi, J., Asherson, P., & Plomin, R. (2008). Evidence for overlapping genetic influences on autistic and ADHD behaviours in a community twin sample. *Journal of Child Psychology and Psychiatry, 49*, 535–542.

Simonoff, E., Pickles, A., Charman, T., Chandler, S., Loucas, T., & Baird, G. (2008). Psychiatric disorders in children with autism spectrum disorders: Prevalence, comorbidity, and associated factors in a population-derived sample. *Journal of the American Academy of Child and Adolescent Psychiatry, 47*, 921–929.

Sowell, E. R., Kan, E., Yoshii, J., Thompson, P. M., Bansal, R., Xu, D., et al. (2008). Thinning of sensorimotor cortices in children with Tourette syndrome. *Nature Neuroscience, 11*, 637–639.

Stein, J. L., Parikshak, N. N., & Geschwind, D. H. (2013). Rare inherited variation in autism: Beginning to see the forest and a few trees. *Neuron, 77*, 209–211.

Stern, E. R., Fitzgerald, K. D., Welsh, R. C., Abelson, J. L., & Taylor, S. F. (2012). Resting-state functional connectivity between fronto-parietal and default mode networks in obsessive-compulsive disorder. *PLoS One, 7*, e36356.

Strömland, K., Nordin, V., Miller, M., Akerström, B., & Gillberg, C. (1994). Autism in Thalidomide embryopathy: A population study. *Developmental Medicine and Child Neurology, 36*, 351–356.

Sucksmith, E., Roth, I., & Hoekstra, R. A. (2011). Autistic traits below the clinical threshold: Re-examining the broader autism phenotype in the 21st century. *Neuropsychology Review, 21*, 360–389.

Turner, K. C., Frost, L., Linsenbardt, D., McIlroy, J. R., & Muller, R. A. (2006). Atypically diffuse functional connectivity between caudate nuclei and cerebral cortex in autism. *Behavioral and Brain Functions, 2*, 34.

Van Steensel, F. J., Bögels, S. M., & de Bruin, E. I. (2013). Psychiatric comorbidity in children with autism spectrum disorders: A comparison with children with ADHD. *Journal of Child and Family Studies, 22*, 368–376.

Zandt, F., Prior, M., & Kyrios, M. (2007). Repetitive behavior in children with high functioning autism and obsessive compulsive disorder. *Journal of Autism and Developmental Disorders, 37*, 251–259.

Part two

The nine degrees of autism

3

The first degree of autism

Being born on the autism spectrum

Michael Fitzgerald and Philip Wylie

> *There is no doubt that all autistic people are born with the condition. It's a genetic condition causing the neurons in the brain not to migrate properly.*
> (Professor Michael Fitzgerald, April 25, 2014)

Introduction

The autistic condition exists before and at birth, despite the fact that it is a developmental disposition that changes over time (Allen et al., 2001). Since autism is really a "developmental condition" rather than a disease (see American Psychiatric Association, 2013) people who are "on the autism spectrum" can lead happy, healthy, meaningful, and successful lives. To do this, though, they need to live in a supportive environment free of prejudice toward people who are different.

The hypothesis for this model

Because we know autism begins in utero (Stoner et al., 2014) the first degree of autism exists in the autistic individual at birth. Therefore, every person on the autism spectrum attains the first degree of autism by the time of his or her birth. Even if an individual with autism dies at birth, he or she will have attained the first degree of autism.

Autism is primarily inherited genetically

Researcher Ami Klin at the Yale Child Study Center supports the notion of autism being a life-long condition. The following is an excerpt from Paul A. Offit's book, *Autism's False Prophets*:

> *Ami Klin found that children with autism, when viewing videotapes of various social situations, didn't focus on the same things as other children. For example, when Klin showed non-autistic children a video of an adult talking, they looked into the adult's eyes. But when Klin showed the same video to autistic children, they didn't look at their eyes; they looked at the mouth. And Klin found these differences when children were only a few weeks old. Hakonarson's and Klin's studies supported the notion that problems with brain wiring occurred during fetal development, not later. These studies are consistent with what many autism researchers had been saying for years – if you're autistic at five, you're autistic at two, and you're autistic at birth.*

(Offit, 2008: Preface page)

The point to recognize from Klin's study is that just because children are diagnosed several years later, or indeed never, it does not mean that they are not on the autism spectrum. Klin also reveals that autism can be suspected shortly after birth (e.g., ASPECT, 2013; Jones & Klin, 2013).

The pioneer of autism research Leo Kanner also concluded that autism is always present at birth and that there is no "cure" for the neurological condition. Leo Kanner wrote in his 1943 article: "We must assume that these children have come into the world with innate physical and intellectual handicaps" (Kanner, 1943: 226). The authors in this book agree that autism begins in utero and is present at birth but do not agree that all autistic children come into the world with innate physical and intellectual handicaps. He also observed similar personality traits in the parents of autistic children, describing them as ". . . cold, bookish, formal, introverted, disdainful of frivolity, humourless, detached and highly – even excessively – rational and objective" (p. 231). This comment, of course, is harsh and insensitive. It's also close to the so-called refrigerated mother idea which

Kanner was initially involved in, although it was propagated by Bruno Bettelheim. Kanner believed that all autistic children are born with the neurological condition, beyond the control of parents and doctors. Some children have severe learning disabilities and others have severe intellectual disability (these are different conditions). Learning disability (e.g., dyslexia, dyscalculia) occurs within the normal IQ range while intellectual disability suggests the individual has below average IQ, usually below 70. Children with IQs of 30 or below may never appreciate they are different from other children or that they have autism. But, we have come to understand that with early intervention and appropriate support, great progress can be made and individuals can lead a comfortable life.

Although autism was first described by Hans Asperger in 1938 and then in 1944 as a personality disorder, parents often like to see it as a condition. We are very aware of the debates regarding terminology, and how individuals respond in different ways to terms such as "condition"; we view autism as a "differing cognitive state" relative to the predominant neurotype.

Parents of children with autism don't like to have it referred to as a disease. Nevertheless to get services or education supports it is necessary to fulfill criteria in *ICD 11* and/or *DSM-V*, which is the international classification of diseases. This currently leaves parents with no choice publicly; if they wish to engage with public services, they need to formally follow the diagnostic terms laid out by such classifications.

In formal psychiatry which deals with conditions that have neurobiological underpinnings the differentiation between condition, personality, and psychiatric disease is blurred. Indeed there is blurring between autistic and neurotypical conditions (i.e., persons without autism). Traits of autism are common with the general population and we only make a diagnosis when a certain threshold of traits is reached. Conditions, in general in psychiatry, exist on spectrums and not in narrow categories. Indeed, neuro-developmental conditions include the following: autism, schizophrenia, bipolar disorder, intellectual disability, ADHD and, as Fitzgerald (2014) has pointed out, some persons with the diagnosis of schizoid personality, narcissistic personality, sadistic personality, and borderline personality can come under the rubric of neuro-developmental disorders too (which is also the category for autism).

Institutional autism is often called autistic-like conditions. These occur in children reared in orphanages for many years without proper food, stimulation, or care. This type of condition is quite different, however, in origin to autism. In many, if not most persons with autism, there are also other conditions as well (e.g., Attention Deficit Disorder with or without hyperactivity (ADHD), Oppositional Defiant Disorder (ODD), Tic Disorder, Obsessive Compulsive Disorder (OCD)). All these comorbid conditions need individual treatments. In terms of etiology many of the comorbid conditions have overlapping etiological features (i.e., from genetic origins). The comorbid conditions are often missed and autism is the only diagnosis given.

Of course, the alternative occurs even more often that people are misdiagnosed with ADHD, OCD, and so on and the autistic diagnosis is missed, which causes massive frustration for the person with autism, the parents, and the treating professions. The features of fetal alcohol syndrome often overlap with autism and the *ICD* criteria for autism are often met (O'Malley, 2013). When the features of autism are met, then the treatments used for autism are appropriate.

The autistic child could develop into a healthy, happy individual if she or he is diagnosed early enough, receives adequate love and support, and has the different way of thinking, which impacts upon behavior, understood. However, without adequate and appropriate intervention, the child faces the risk of developing secondary psychiatric conditions such as depression and other forms of mental illness (Attwood, 2007).

Autistic savant photographer Danny Beath (1960–Jan. 2014) said:

I believe I was born with these qualities and they are the core abilities that have helped me develop life-long skills as an adult. It almost seems I was born with a very special 'song' that all the other 'birds' lacked. It is the 'ugly duckling' or 'nightingale' syndrome, in which an outwardly ordinary creature has a hidden ability that enables it to shine above the others when stimulated. This creates tension and jealousies amongst its peers and always leads to teasing and bullying.

Professional autism counselor Louise Page who comes from a multi-generational family of people on the spectrum believes that:

True autism is predominantly a part of the genetic makeup of an individual, which is not only present at birth, but is a characteristic or addition to an individual's being which may have travelled like an angelic passenger in the genes through the generations, becoming an intrinsic part of the individual when first conceived.

(Personal communication, November 15, 2013)

Louise also states that genetically inherited autism is not exclusively passed to the child from the father's genes during conception. The lineage of the autism spectrum can also be continued through the genes of the mother. When there is strong evidence of the presence of the autism spectrum in family groups and generations, either or both of the male or female lineages contribute to autism's possible continuation (see Causes of autism in References).

Counter claims to the idea that autism exists at birth?

Although autism is primarily a genetic condition, some researchers believe that toxins, other genetic material, or excess testosterone in the mother's uterus occasionally impacts upon the condition (Baron-Cohen et al., 2011). But, by whatever route our autism takes, if it is not inherited directly via the parents' genes, the condition would have developed in utero, so it is *always* present at birth.

Professor Tony Attwood says:

I am not sure whether all cases of autism are caused genetically. It is often a genetic component or something becomes toxic to affect brain development. We also suspect that health issues during pregnancy including antibodies and auto-immune disorders may cause autism.

(Attwood, 2007)

Attwood recognizes three distinct pathways that contribute to autism:

1. Genetic inheritance of autism at conception
2. Genetic material that causes autism (before birth)
3. Toxins in utero that affect the child's brain development

In the first case, when the baby inherits autism, there is usually a clear family line of autism and possibly other psychiatric conditions. Investigation of the parents' ancestry can bring useful information, especially for parents of autistic children who want to know about the likelihood of having another autistic child. This is what geneticists call "penetration of the family line." If the genetic markers are identified, our concern is that a eugenics approach of racial cleansing might be taken by eliminating potential geniuses of the future. Most of the people who made major advances in art and science have Aspergic characteristics (a form of high-functioning autism). To be successful as a species we need neuro-diversity. If we use an analogy with Star Trek, "we need Balkans" (Professor Tony Attwood, personal communication, October 24, 2013).

There are, however, several dubious claims that autism is associated with post-natal elements (e.g., via mercury or vaccinations) – but, to date, research doesn't support these claims.

Offit's (2008) book *Autism's False Prophets: Bad Science, Risky Medicine and the Search for the Cure* is a condemnation of a large group of parents, journalists, researchers, and activists who believe that autism is a disease that needs curing. This book debunks the myth that autism is caused by vaccine poisoning. Since writing his book, Dr. Offit says he has received a massive amount of hate mail and even death threats.

Psychiatrists Leo Kanner and Bruno Bettelheim initially believed that "refrigerator parents" were the primary cause of autism but this theory was later overturned. This is an incredibly harsh and brutal statement by Kanner. Kanner did blame the parents, which led to the false ideology of "refrigerator mother" of autism. This was taken up by Bruno Bettelheim and many psychoanalysts with tragic consequences for many years. This became one of the great tragic stories in the history of psychiatry, which has so many tragic stories including prefrontal lobotomy, malaria treatment, dousing in freezing water, and so on. Kanner later changed his mind about the etiology and said parents were not to blame but he said it was much too late then and the damage had been done.

Autism's "false prophets" also cite trauma, allergies, drug abuse, mercury, laziness, and existential angst as possibly playing a role in the development of the autism condition.

The Autism Research Centre published the following notice on its website,

We have been testing if foetal testosterone, measured in amniotic fluid obtained via amniocentesis, is associated with later psychological and neural development post-natally.

We have conducted studies of typical individual differences and found that foetal testosterone is inversely associated with social development, language development, and empathy; and that foetal testosterone is positively associated with systemizing and a number of autistic traits.

The rationale for testing foetal testosterone comes from animal studies, which suggest this hormone, prenatally, masculinizes the brain. Given the sex ratio in autism and Asperger Syndrome, and the masculinized cognitive profile reported in studies of empathy and systemizing in people with these diagnoses, foetal testosterone may be an important candidate biological mechanism to help understand the phenotype.

Whether or not fetal testosterone is a significant cause of Asperger's syndrome or autism, it definitely occurs prenatally.

Autism is a spectrum of varying ability and developmental delay

There is usually a delay between the first degree of autism and the second degree of autism, when the child becomes aware of his or her "differences." It's not usually possible to identify autism at birth as diagnosis is based upon behavioral observation rather than genetic testing. However, parents often have suspicions about autism in the first year of life of the child especially those who have had other children with or without autism. They may be very quick to notice the difference or the similarity if they have had another child already with autism.

Although autism may be suspected before the first year of life (e.g., Casanova, 2006; Jones & Klin, 2013), usually the earliest age that an autistic child is diagnosed is around 18 months of age. However, unfortunately, usually identification occurs several years later while the child is at primary school (Attwood, 2004).

Christa Wilson refers to the delay in awareness of the autistic condition:

We were born without awareness of our autistic genes or our parents' autistic genes. This is extremely noticeable in late-diagnosis as autism is still relatively young in the field of pathological research and especially the genetic link. For some children, there was an obvious difference from birth, such as with my brother, but even those who suffer late diagnosis due to the slowly emerging understanding of the condition in our generation, would have been considered 'slow' or 'special' (having a learning disability) so no further investigation would be made.

(Personal communication, January 2014)

Some key characteristics in autism genetics

The key characteristics to look out for while conducting genetic penetration of the family line are social awkwardness, lonesomeness, inflexibility, and resistance to change with a preference for fixed routines, susceptibility to sensory overload including noise and crowds, autistic features that lead to sleeping in separate beds and the use of sleeping tablets for insomnia, depression, introversion, indirect eye contact, unduly direct communication, relationship issues, inability to sustain employment, and limited cognitive empathy if an individual isn't interested or attached (Fitzgerald, 2005).

When investigating the family ancestry for various conditions, a very strong law of attraction usually becomes apparent. This law of attraction brings together people who are on the autism spectrum and individuals who have other hidden neurological conditions. For example, an individual with autism may attract individuals who have other issues such as learning difficulty (e.g., dyspraxia, dyslexia, ADD) or individuals who have similar features to themselves.

Researchers at John Hopkins Bloomberg School of Public Health suggested that some prenatal use of Selective Serotonin Reuptake Inhibitors (SSRIs) by mothers to treat depression causes autistic presentation and developmental delays in their male babies. If the condition caused by the mother's use of anti-depressants is actually autism, it would have existed before birth (Harrington et al., 2014).

Alternatively, the toxins affecting the fetus may be adverse prenatal environmental factors causing similar traits to autism in the baby.

Other neurological conditions, such as Attachment Disorder, give rise to similar traits as autism. Attachment Disorder is caused by a lack of bonding between the baby and carer. This may be considered as an adverse environmental factor which likely intensifies the child's presentation if he or she has autism and/or can mirror autism.

A major diagnostic pathway for autism and other hidden neurological conditions is identification of autism in an individual's child or another family member. Executive Director of GRASP Michael John Carley received a diagnosis for Asperger's syndrome after his son was identified as being on the autism spectrum. This meant that Michael's son was never alone exploring his condition because father and son took the journey together (Carley, 2008).

When asked how many fathers of autistic sons are willing to be assessed for the same condition, Michael estimates about 40 percent. The remaining 60 percent may or may not understand the condition and be capable of supporting their child through it, because they prefer not to identify with the autistic personally.

Denial of autism by parents and other relatives is common because the condition is genetically inherited and because it is potentially embarrassing, provoking stigmas that are unjust. Most of Michael's family did not want him to seek a diagnosis, and some wanted him to keep the outcome a secret. Michael says:

> *'We have to remember that, because of the genetics involved, and because of the new interpretations of the past that will have to be explored, we are not the only ones affected by our diagnosis.*
>
> (Personal communication, November 16, 2012)

Unfortunately, denial by the autistic person's family exacerbates family problems and may lead to mental illness. However, when the parents are able to courageously accept their genetic disposition and overcome their denial, they can strengthen intra-familial relationships.

There are many barriers to self-identification and subsequent self-acceptance of autism by parents. The main obstacles to self-identification and diagnosis of parents are:

- Fear of the mental health system
- Unfair stigmas relating to neurological conditions
- Prejudice toward autistic people (often based on a misunderstanding of autism itself)
- Misinformation about the condition
- Inflexibility
- Confused association between autism, criminality, and psychopathy
- Belief that autism is insanity
- Confusion between autism and mental illness
- Focus on impairments rather than gifts (or simply differences)
- Falsely believing that autism is a disease rather than a developmental disposition
- Lack of belief in the existence of autism

Similarly, many parents will be autistic themselves though unidentified and unacknowledged. In some cases, the similarities between parent and offspring may cause problems. For example – the assumption by the parent being: "Well, I am like that and I'm not autistic, so therefore you can't be either." This difficulty is so common. I've been told many times, "You don't seem autistic to me." Then there's, "Well, we all have a bit of autism in us; you are no different to me." This sentence to me is accusatory and implies I need to be ashamed of either not being autistic enough or of being too autistic. Being born anatomically female also gives rise to a different pattern of autism which is often over looked (Wenn Lawson, personal communication, 2014).

Dr. Luke Beardon (2012) comments about the prevailing misinformation about autism:

> Ok, now I am not suggesting that in modern times people are still suggesting that autism is a mental illness or a disease (please don't tell me if they are, there's only so much ignorance a person can take). BUT – if this is the case, why are sets of criteria to be found in the International Classification of **DISEASES** and in the tome published by the American **PSYCHIATRIC** Association?
>
> Why do people often get referred to a **PSYCHIATRIST** for a diagnosis, why are children often referred to Child and Adolescent **MENTAL HEALTH** Services (when there is no mental health issues evident)? I am not suggesting for one moment that

there are not good psychiatrists or mental health professionals out there, but what 'qualifies' them to work with autistic folk? Surely, the erroneous connotations twixt autism and mental illness/disease are not safe, nor sensible.

Leo Gregory of ANCA comments about genetic pathways or bloodlines:

In every family that we worked with, you can see the (autistic) traits (among other family members). You can see the communication similarities. Whether the parents understand it, or not, is irrelevant. But when we put them through a training program where they have to understand themselves before we even work with the child, they start to see the pattern.
(Personal communication, November 21, 2013)

The fact that autism is present at or before birth means that there is nearly always a delay before the individual is diagnosed as being on the autism spectrum. Why? Only in exceptional circumstances would diagnosticians identify a baby as being on the autism spectrum at birth. Professor Michael Fitzgerald claims that he can identify autism in babies as young as two years old. This means that the majority of individuals who are on the autism spectrum have a delayed diagnosis.

When psychologist Dr. Wenn Lawson was asked whether he came across any cases where autism is not genetically inherited, he replied:

I have, but it's not very often that that happens. There's an autism disposition born out of traumatic brain injury (which can cause) autism-like behaviour. There is also some evidence that viral damage can cause autism-like behaviours and/or severe deprivation can mimic autism but the majority of cases are caused genetically.
(Personal communication, 2012)

Although in this developmental model every autistic individual begins life as an autistic being, not all autistic people reach the second degree of autism (being aware that they are different from neuro-typical people). Some babies with autism die at, or shortly after, birth, while others may die later in childhood before being aware of their differences.

Professor Simon Baron-Cohen says:

We know that autism is not 100% genetic in origin, since in the case of identical twins (who share 100% of their genes), there are instances of one twin having autism and the other not having it. In fact, the likelihood of the co-twin also having autism where one of them has it (in monozygotic (MZ) pairs) is about 60%. This means that there must be some non-genetic (i.e., environmental) factors that are part of the cause of autism.

However, this does not mean that the adverse environmental factors that contribute to the autistic condition are post-natal. The presence of toxins, excess testosterone, and even professional negligence during birth may be labeled as environmental factors during pregnancy up until delivery (see: Causes of autism in References).

Although we can concur autism appears to be due to a combination of genetic and environmental factors, it is generally unclear which genetic and which environmental factors are important. About 5–10% of autism cases involve a single severe genetic defect or disorder, such as Fragile X or tuberous sclerosis, and many of those individuals develop the characteristics of autism. However, 90–95% of cases do not involve a single severe defect, but instead appear to involve a complex set of many genetic variations and environmental factors (see: Causes of autism in References).

Diagnostic issues

Many would argue the problem is that diagnosis is based upon observation. This requires expert assessment but it also requires the individual be in a place, with a sense of his or her own autonomy, where the individual can be "himself or herself." If the individual has learning disability or/and intellectual disability, the person is less likely to be able to mask difficulties. But for those with high-functioning autism, masking may have become a way of life (Holliday-Willey, 1999).

So, autism as a genetic condition causes the neurons in the brain not to migrate properly (Fitzgerald, personal communication, April 25, 2014). It also demonstrates smaller brain mini-columns than we see in typical development (see: Causes of autism in References).

These brain differences will cause individuals with autism to have difficulties with understanding others, difficulties with communication and emotional expression. But, they will also cause focused attention and a narrowing of interests. This can be a bonus in many areas of vocation where such expertise is helpful.

Autism is NOT madness but a disability (Fitzgerald, personal communication, April 25, 2014). However, we do not consider all autistic individuals as disabled, but acknowledge that almost all will be disadvantaged.

"I do not consider autism as a form of insanity," Dr. Neel Burton, Psychiatrist (2012).

Summary

Every individual with autism is born with the condition *without exception*. This means that every autistic individual who is born alive achieves the first degree of autism.

The first degree autistic individual is not aware that he or she is different from other children. Typically, the autistic children become aware of their differences between the age of six and twelve years old; this stage is termed, the second degree of autism. However, the autistic child's parents or other people such as medical doctors may be aware that the child is not "typical" during first degree autism.

The first degree autistic child is not mentally ill. Mental illness is caused by detrimental external environmental factors *after* the child becomes aware that he or she is different from most other children. When mental illness is of a genetic disposition it is usually triggered in the middle teens (e.g., schizophrenia).

Louise Page also states there may be an unconscious or conscious awareness, depending upon age and developmental stage of the individuals, based in an instinctual acknowledgment of "difference" among such persons. For those persons who are more aware of their "difference," sharing personal and general life experiences associated with being on the autism spectrum and/or other neurological conditions can be cathartic and may provide a bonding, be supportive and offer an affiliated understanding of their ways of being.

Page says that for some of those individuals living with persistent denial of their own autism disposition causes difficulties accepting changes to perhaps a life-long experience and perspective of trying to "fit in" (personal communication, 2013). They may perhaps feel that changes to their beliefs and concepts of self may elicit fears, apprehension, self-doubt (of past self as they have understood such) and so on, and such changes may feel too formidable to face. Fears of how such issues may affect self, family, and other connections may be another perceived obstacle in personal acceptance and recognition of being an individual with autism. Though, some persons can experience a feeling of liberation when a recognition or diagnosis of self seems to fill in all the "gaps" of understanding one's self, and possibly others, in the past and present times.

Although there is no "cure" or medical treatment for autism, most people on the autism spectrum would not want to be neuro-typical. Autistic individuals are "wired differently" in their brains causing unique thinking and behavior. Therefore, the autistic community is essentially a different culture which is extremely diverse.

As a neurological condition, autism gives rise to both gifts and difficulties, relative to the neuro-typical population. However, some support – or at least protection from abuse – is normally required for the child to manifest his or her gifts.

However, with the main method used to diagnose autism being observation only, unfortunately, because so few people properly understand autism and the condition is so diverse, some believe many go undiagnosed (Wylie & Heath, 2013), while many others remain unrecognized (Fitzgerald, 2014).

The path from first to second degree autism

Usually, without understanding why, the child with high-functioning autism becomes aware that he or she is different to typical children, between the ages of six and twelve.

There is always a delay between the first degree of autism and the second degree of autism, when the child becomes aware of his or her "differences," because it is not usually possible to identify autism at birth as diagnosis is based upon behavioral observation rather than genetic testing. Early intervention needs to take place before the final definitive diagnosis. The best outcome is where there is intensive early intervention.

References

Allen, D.A., Steinberg, M., Dunn, M., Fein, D., Feinstein, C., Waterhouse, L., et al. (2001). Autistic disorder versus other pervasive developmental disorders in young children: Same or different? *European Child and Adolescent Psychiatry, 10,* 67–78.

American Psychiatric Association. (2013). *Diagnostic and statistical manual of mental disorders* (5th ed.). Washington, DC: Author.

ASPECT. (2013). Frequently asked questions: Diagnosis. Retrieved from http://www.autismspectrum.org.au/content/diagnosis

Attwood, T. (2004, June 20). Interview on *Sixty Minutes*. Retrieved from http://sixtyminutes.ninemsn.com.au/webchats/263824/breaking-point-professor-tony-attwood

Attwood, T. (2007). *The complete guide to Asperger's syndrome.* London: Jessica Kingsley Publishers.

Baron-Cohen, S., Lombardo, M.V., Auyeung, B., Ashwin, E., Chakrabarti, B., & Knickmeyer, R. (2011). Why are autism spectrum conditions more prevalent in males? *PLoS Biology.* Retrieved from www.plosbiology.org

Beardon, L. (2012, April). The myths of autism. Asperger's United, No. 70. Retrieved from www.autisticrightsmovementuk.org/pages/mythsofautism.pdf

Beath, Danny. (2013). Asperger's syndrome: Evolutionary advantages of Asperger's syndrome. *Awares* . Retrieved from http://awares.nemisys.uk.com/conferences/show_paper.asp?section=000100010001&conferenceCode=000200020002&id=54

Burton, N. (2012). *Psychology Today.* Retrieved from https://www.psychologytoday.com/

Carley, M.J. (2008). *Asperger's from the inside out.* New York: Perigee Books.

Casanova M. F. (2006). Neuropathological and genetic findings in autism: the significance of a putative minicolumnopathy, *The NeuroScientist, 12*(5):435–441.

Fitzgerald, M. (2005). *The genesis of artistic creativity: Asperger syndrome and the arts.* London: Jessica Kingsley Publishers.

Fitzgerald, M. (2014). Retrieved from http://professormichaelfitzgerald.eu/

Harrington, R., et al. (2014). *Johns Hopkins Bloomberg School of Public Health researchers find association between SSRI use during pregnancy and autism and developmental delays in boys.* Retrieved from http://www.jhsph.edu/news/news-releases/2014/ johns-hopkins-bloomberg-school-of-public-health-researchers-find-association-between-ssri-use-during-pregnancy-and-autism-and-developmental-delays-in-boys.html.

Holliday-Willey, L. (1999). *Pretending to be normal.* London: Jessica Kingsley.

Jones, W., & Klin, A. (2013, November 6). Attention to eyes is present but in decline in 2–6-month-old infants later diagnosed with autism. *Nature, 504*(7480): 427–431. doi:10.1038/nature12715

Kanner, L. (1943). Autistic disturbances of affective contact. *Nervous Child, 2,* 217–250.

Offit, P. (2008). *Autism's false prophets: Bad science, risky medicine, and the search for a cure.* New York: Columbia University Press.

O'Malley, K. (2013). Clinical implications of a link between fetal alcohol spectrum disorders and autism or Asperger's disorder – A neurodevelopmental frame for helping, understanding and management. In M. Fitzgerald (Ed.), *Recent advances in autism spectrum disorders* (Vol. 1, pp. 451–476). Rijeka, Croatia: InTech.

Stoner, R., Chow, M. L., Boyle, M. O., Susan M. Sunkin, S. M.,. Mouton, P. R., Roy, S. et al. (2014). Patches of disorganization in the neocortex of children with autism. *New England Journal of Medicine, 370,* 1209–1219.

Wylie, P., & Heath, S. (2013). *Very late diagnosis of Asperger's syndrome 2013 UK Survey.* Retrieved from http://goo.gl/kvKGG0

Web Information

Autism Research Centre: http://www.autismresearchcentre.com/

Causes of autism:

http://thechart.blogs.cnn.com/2014/07/22/genetics-play-a-bigger-role-than-environmental-causes-for-autism

http://www.nhs.uk/news/2014/10October/Pages/Autism-genes-details-uncovered-in-global-study.aspx?app_data=%7b%22pi%2 2:%2257840_1414689957_1656409592%22%2c%22pt%22:%22 twitter%22%7d

http://minicolumn.org/people/casanova/

http://thechart.blogs.cnn.com/2014/07/22/genetics-play-a-bigger-role-than-environmental-causes-for-autism/
http://www.autism.com/understanding_advice
http://www.jhsph.edu/news/news-releases/2014/johns-hopkins-bloomberg-school-of-public-health-researchers-find-association-between-ssri-use-during-pregnancy-and-autism-and-develop mental-delays-in-boys.html

4

The second degree of autism

Knowing that we are different, without understanding why

Louise Page

Introduction

The individual on the autism spectrum attains the second degree of autism when becoming aware that he or she is different from others who may be considered "neuro-typical" (NT). The journey to uncover this, though, is different for us all. This chapter attempts to paint the picture of such a journey.

During the second degree of autism, the individual notices his or her different traits without understanding them or their causation. The autistic person may not become fully aware of the neurological condition until he or she has reached the fourth degree of autism – "*Self-identification*."

While many autistic individuals are aware of being different during the second degree of autism, they do not judge these differences in any way which is discernible to others or self. Moreover, the individual may not judge his or her unique traits until the individual attains the third degree of autism – "*Struggling to fit into society (and possibly pretending to be normal)*."

Hypothesis for this model

As individuals grow through childhood from infancy, the opportunities and occurrences of potentially becoming aware of "difference" to their peers increases. This may be determined by the child's own developmental stage of self-awareness and ability to understand the concept of difference. Even though this is the child's "nature" from birth, it's only seen as "a difference" at this stage. It's as this awareness develops and moves a person into the third degree of autism that awareness of difference turns to pain.

Sometimes self-awareness of "difference" may not be the initial impacting element. The first element of consciousness of "difference" can be when others, such as peers or adults, treat one with disregard, avoidance, teasing, or alienation from a group environment. This can be a time when one is witness to criticism or disrespectful comments from familiar or unfamiliar persons. Sometimes this comes from within the greater family circle and sometimes parent/carer targeted. The potential impact of such behaviors of others, combined with increased self-perceptions, can be the beginning of a personal journey for the child with autism leading to confusion about his or her real self.

The hypothesis for nine degrees of autism states we are each born on the autism spectrum, but, many of us don't recognize this for some time. It's only during the second degree of autism that autistic children perceive themselves as being the ones who are different.

Reaching awareness in second degree autism may take many years for some, while others take less time. For example, the autistic child may feel that the other children are the ones who behave strangely (e.g., B. J. Lazones, aged 17 diagnosed with autism aged 2). There are autistic people who perceived themselves as being more intelligent than their peers. Of course, this is a form of second degree autism (i.e., feeling different but in a positive way). However, this side of the individual may not be appreciated by others who view them as being insensitive to others.

The personal experience, perceptions of self and others, and when and why a person on the autism spectrum may feel he or she is different to his or her peers will be discussed in this chapter. Also, parental observations and the personal experiences of individuals on the spectrum will be explored.

Body awareness

The moments of discovery of when one perceives his or her difference from others can be as diverse as the individuality of the person himself or herself. I once described a "sum of one's being" as being synonymous with a fluid mathematical equation, with the components of such an equation being:

- personality,
- gene memory and inheritance,
- physical, intellectual, emotional, and psychological health and abilities,
- environmental influences,
- sense of well-being and safety, nurturing received and sustenance, and so on.

So a consideration of the above eclectic mix of life experiences and way of being can help in the understanding of how, when, and why an autistic individual may become aware of being different to others.

An understanding of the typical stages of human development is imperative when achieving clarity regarding the true knowledge of one's difference to another. Such awareness, though at a subconscious level, can begin within one's psyche as young as infancy, perhaps just beyond the stages of actively noticing and interacting with one's environment. Being receptive to the behavior and attention of people around you is a developmental process, so often delayed in autism. Six months is an approximate age of such awareness, though this varies depending on the disposition of the infant.

Before this landmark stage an instinctual and primal need for bonding emotionally and physically with the birth mother is the first introduction to natural communication with the world as we will come to know it. This is a crucial time of interacting with, being affected by, and responding to one's environment. Interplaying with this experience is the inherent disposition of the infant himself or herself.

Such primal communication and natural disposition provide the first signals to self and others that the world is a comfortable place to be. However, venturing into the world where receptive and expressive messages about how we fit may be littered with fractured signs and meanings is uncomfortable. Sometimes confusion and distress interrupt this process and suggest to some individuals a sense of not belonging and of being in a foreign land.

The first sign

Some children will have aversion to touch, sounds, or general nurturing activities and environmental elements. This leaves parents very confused, worried, upset and, in some cases, feeling that the natural bonding experience may not be achievable. This moment in time can be the first sign of difficulties which correlate with a future diagnosis of autism. Thus begins the journey through childhood of perceiving and being considered as an individual of "difference" to peers, parents, and others.

Recoiling from sounds, people, touch, and other sensorial experiences is considered overreactive by a parent/carer or other observer. Though distress is recognized by the observer, it is also innately registered by the child's subconscious. This recognition of a personally impacting environment affects comfort ability and constantly nags at a child's awareness.

When one collates the two experiences (the observer and the child's own impressions of an event), a conclusion the child is feeling a difference, an aversion to his or her environment and the parent acknowledging such, is an initial sign. This means the child may be enduring the first primary indicators of being on the autism spectrum. This is confirmed via an eclectic mix of autistic behaviors seen at time of formal diagnosis of autism.

Observations

The young child, whether being held in the carer's arms or playing in solitude, may be seen by others as the silent observer; the one who is seen as an "old soul" who may not respond to others. However, he or she may be quietly sensing and absorbing the fascinating, strange, or undesired activity of events and people around him or her.

Some persons perceive the child who is not facing or looking at them as one who is not listening. Such perception implies communication problems, a lack of responsiveness. This is suggestive of cocoon-like properties excluding all around them. Just as autism is considered a spectrum regarding each unique individual, there is also a range or spectrum of how each autistic person will communicate with others. This includes the environment and its influence upon one's sense of difference.

Whereas the quiet, reserved, and apparently non-conventional communicative soul is at one end of the spectrum, there are other young autistic persons who are openly expressive and communicate their intentions or feelings in an obvious manner. Again, there may be a varied range of the volume, intensity, manner, and behaviors as to how such is expressed.

Such displays and meaning of expression combine with fluctuating degrees of emotion. All autistic persons feel and express emotion in a way commensurate with the "sum of their being," environmental, health, and emotional influences in the moment.

The range of affect the awareness of "difference" has on the autistic individual can be as variable as the autism presentation itself. This depends on the person's life experiences. The child's self-perceived differences often lead to solitary activity, while avoidance by others may reinforce the child's feeling of being different from others. The child's perception of differences is instinctual and intuitive, creating the foundations of the individual's self-identity. Naturally, how the child judges these differences may directly affect his or her self-esteem and worth to self, others, and the wider community.

As an example, a young girl living with high-functioning autism (previously known as Asperger's syndrome) may join with individuals in her life in a manner perceived as typical for her peer group, style, and developmental age/stage. She may sense she is different but not to such an extent that such a "difference" impacts negatively on her daily life. This can continue through childhood and into teenage years. For some there is a growing desire to socialize on a one-to-one basis with a like-minded and/or accepting friend, rather than be part of a group. During these years of greater self-awareness the nature of a young person can build an awareness of acceptance, or not, by peers. This enhances or detracts from the challenges surrounding them. This is when the awareness of their difference presents challenges for individuals in school, home, social, and various other environments.

Pertinent to the examination and understanding of when an individual begins to feel different are the observations of the parent/carers, teachers, friends, family, or professionals involved in the daily life of the autistic person.

Such observations of emerging awareness of "difference" by the individual could include the following points. Some of these points are more relevant to the developmental age and stage of a very young individual, while others are more applicable to the behaviors of an older person. Alternatively, many of the points of observation listed below apply to a broad range of ages regarding the autistic person's emerging or established awareness experiences.

While the individual's appreciation of difference is being noted, others will read his or her body language, verbal responses, and/or emotional state and so on.

Reactions in younger children

Younger children with emerging awareness display certain reactions when they:

- Watch others play at a distance, while quietly and silently sitting away from the group, perhaps staring directly at or looking at them from an angle.
- Attempt to join with their peers, but are rejected, ignored, or ridiculed.
- Hide, run away, or turn their back on the others.
- Avoid groups, noisy rooms or others, busy areas, or highly cluttered rooms.
- Run or move swiftly away from sudden sounds. Physically shudder and express emotion and behaviors (physical or verbal) – perhaps unable to settle again (sensory overload with accompanying unique responses).
- Display embarrassment, fear, or catatonia when feeling challenged by the environment or others.
- Outwardly express (verbally and/or physically) themselves which may spoil others' games, belongings, or activities due to frustration, anger, or rejection. Some, on the other hand, may be called the "spoiler" as they may overly exert their energies in an attempt to join in, perhaps without understanding the social rules of the group. Some other individuals may join the group, but be involved quietly.
- Be conscious of not being invited to parties, sleep-overs, play-dates, and so on.

Though the above points are limited as examples, they highlight some scenarios where the young autistic person is involved in communal settings and the challenges associated with "difference" can become evident.

Response to awareness

When a young individual is vividly aware of feeling "different," imitation of others to "fit in" can become emotionally taxing. Many autistic persons come to realize that this feels unnatural to them and may choose to express their real self. This leads to potential implications like ridicule from others and increased emotional distress. Alternatively, this self-initiated freedom to be one's self can result, for some, in feeling liberated and unconcerned about how others perceive them. An adventure into this new realm of "self" relieves many tensions they have felt when being untrue to their innate self.

For some autistic persons there is longevity in such satisfaction. But for others this can be the beginning of feelings of difference causing derision, a lack of acceptance, and feeding a process that is ultimately self-defeating. The implications of this outcome may be a retreat into one's "self" or a tendency for regression to past anxious behaviors.

Other autistic persons have successfully been enabled to embrace and be proud of their individuality and "difference." They confidently and perhaps avidly deflect any negativity towards them by others. This may apply to those individuals who, although at first thought their difference was due to being very intelligent, have positively gone on in life to ultimately use their intelligence productively.

Solidarity with one's real "self" and the newly acquired nurtured self-confidence is further enhanced when the autistic person has total support. Such understanding, unconditional caring, love, and acceptance from the most important people in their lives is essential. This quality base is even further enhanced when an autistic person is able to feel such positivity from the world around him or her.

Positive experiences

So, as you can see not all interrelating experiences are negative for the autistic child. Many group activities can elicit pleasant feelings. When experiences connect like-minded, empathetic peers and others to understanding these are welcoming and supportive.

Through observing the young autistic person's responses to his or her environment, one can see the child is experiencing a stage of development where the child is reacting to certain challenges.

Feelings and emotions are telling the child one thing, but the child doesn't have the intellectual understanding to appreciate what it all means, so the child's "story" of autism begins to emerge.

The older autistic individual is better equipped to express feelings of difference than when he or she was a child. The individual is either aware of his or her autism or able to recognize when and how the emotions surrounding the feeling of difference impact his or her life. Some individuals realize when the following points are at odds with them, for example:

- Some have a conscious awareness of their disregard or disinterest in following fashions, peer trends, or social behaviors, compared to the importance others give them.
- Some aim to maintain and be true to their individuality. This experience may range from levels of high anxiety all the way through to self-acceptance and pride.
- There may be an aversion to small talk or cluster conversations or perceived meaningless discussions.
- For others, a preference to converse with precise information and topics versus conversations littered with innuendos and irrelevance to personal interests is shown.
- At times, groups, busy or noisy public places are intimidating or just not preferred for sensory or other personal reasons.
- Many form relationships but the difficulty with making friends can be limiting. This might be due to not sharing similar interests, or the autistic person may have some ongoing anxieties about social "rules." The individual experiences emotional difficulties if the individual sees or perceives others to be achieving harmonious relationships seamlessly and with confidence.
- It will be difficult when expectations and demands to follow others contradict personal beliefs and desires.
- When rules in the workplace, school, or other environments are unclear or leave the individual feeling that he or she doesn't conform like everyone else, the individual may experience difficulties or misunderstandings.
- When an individual witnesses others frustrated with his or her ways (mannerisms and so on), then embarrassment, anxieties, frustration, anger, sadness, or distress can follow. When feeling that another person is annoyed with him or her but showing little

empathy, the autistic person is left disconcerted and doubting his or her own abilities.

Depending on the nature and general character of the autistic person, the self-confidence and esteem afforded that person, he or she may hide awareness of feeling different. The person may feel he or she doesn't fit in and doesn't want to expose these thoughts and associated emotions. This, in effect, is also a form of self-denial as well as a deep uncertainty about the social and community value to one's self and others. With such an avoidance of accepting one's way of being, elements of depression, anxiety, and sadness may present and/ or increase. How an autistic individual is regarded by others is also an influencing factor in such self-imposed beliefs and responses.

Other situations which arise for some older autistic persons are the manifestations of comorbid conditions such as depression, obsessive compulsive behaviors, and other psychological or emotional conditions. The timeline between second degree autism and third degree autism, when the individual struggles to fit into society, varies according to his or her environmental conditions including access to support. The autistic individual who suffers in an adverse environment would attain third degree autism before those who live in more favorable environments. Bad environments often bring the individual to a questioning place and opens doors to moving on to third degree autism.

The litmus test for environmental conditions is whether the autistic person can survive without undue social "punishment" when *being* his or her self. This means that an autistic child who lives in an abusive environment is unlikely to express himself or herself without considerable bullying or chastisement. Such adverse environments are likely to push the autistic individual into third degree autism.

Dr. Wenn Lawson says that many children reach second degree autism as early as seven years old but it varies.

Some kids can be seven or eight and already talking about suicide because they know they don't fit. I still think that you can have a sort of an awareness that you're not the same as other kids even among three or four year olds, but they don't have a word for it or they can't explain it. It's a feeling state when they don't feel comfortable. But awareness and being able to put it

65

into some form of understanding would really depend on the child's IQ, background, family and communication style among other things. You couldn't really say by the age of this or by that because there are too many factors. But it would be a growing awareness for sure.

(Personal communication, 2013)

Maxine Aston states:

There are reasons why the child becomes aware around the twelve year mark. Yes I agree it is a crime and in a way abusive to not educate the child on the way they are unique and process information differently. 'Theory of mind' does not kick in with people affected by autism till between the years of 9–14 years and this is the time that the majority of my clients notice a change in their perception of themselves and others. In typical children 'Theory of mind' develops from the age of three.

(Happe & Frith, 1995: 196)

Louise Page states she has witnessed children on the spectrum as young as four years old who may be conscious of their peers avoiding them, particularly children who are sensitive to the responses and feelings of others. However, the child's awareness of being different from others can become increasingly intense up until and beyond the teenage years.

These emotional and psychological challenges can continue on into adulthood where obstacles to happiness and well-being continue to be faced due to the ignorance of others and to a non-supportive environment. For some, aiming to reach personal autonomy may be akin to riding a roller coaster. Of course, parental communication of one's differences is not the only important aspect to the child discovering he or she is on the autism spectrum. The child may also begin asking questions as to why he or she feels different or why he or she is being treated differently by others.

It can come like an epiphany. An autistic person, who may not be formally diagnosed, begins to suspect his or her way of being himself or herself is causing reactions in others. The heartache which comes from this soul-felt feeling can be the point from which the individual begins to ask "why" these experiences are being encountered. Some, who have previously been confident by degrees with their social, emotional, and interactive abilities, begin to question themselves, others, and at worst, the whole of their life existence in general.

The realization that they have lived a life till now without being fully aware of their relationship to the autism spectrum causes a mild to severe shift in one's self-confidence and overall well-being. Some feel that all of those years past, with a varying amount of frustrations, social difficulties, emotional slumps and highs, feeling alienated from peer groups and so on, may have not been necessary if they could have known more about their unique way of being in the earlier days of their life. If they had been given the opportunity to work through and conquer fears, doubts, and other experiences which have left them feeling there was something different with them, personal difficulties would have been lessened or greatly alleviated. All along, there was really nothing "wrong" with them; they had just not discovered all of their "right."

Some individuals feel overwhelmed with fear, uncertainty, sadness, and self-doubt, much like the process of grief. The opportunity for emotionally adverse behaviors to surreptitiously emerge to complicate this new learning about one's self can present a difficult and lengthy series of processes to be worked through.

Yet other individuals may welcome this new knowledge as the answer to all of the lurking questions they have previously had about themselves. So one individual will feel despair and yet, at the other extreme, another individual will feel freed and achieve the greatest sense of self and unique individuality, embraced with pride.

Maintaining a clear vision of the personal goals to achieve understanding and acceptance of self can be a challenge. Some find this in the short term while for others it takes a lifetime. The quality of emotional, psychological, physical, professional and family support, understanding, and respect is crucial to the well-being of the autistic person.

The range of individual responses to such a discovery, realization, and increased awareness of the true self is as vast as the spectrum of autism. Many individuals also find they will now be experiencing a huge array of mixed emotions, as they aim to grasp or attain clarity.

Other important aspects of how one responds to the realization of "difference" to others are the verbal and physical expressions of the feelings surrounding such, and this includes how one's coping mechanisms are observed by others.

The author of this model (nine degrees of autism), Philip Wylie, managed to be successful during his education and even completed a master's degree. During Philip's education, he was offered a great deal of space to explore, experiment, and to be himself. During his secondary school education, he began to feel different from other children, but he attributed this to higher intelligence, so he had a positive self-image while he experienced second degree autism. However, when he began employment in the "real world" without any meaningful support, he experienced third degree autism with confusion and poor mental health.

Children who live in a safe and supportive environment with genuine unconditional love are most likely to be able to express themselves authentically – which may appear quirky to normal people. They do so without fear of ridicule or embarrassment. Children who live in controlled environments are most likely to "shut down" emotionally and withdraw into themselves.

Autism mentor Sara Heath (personal communication with Phil Wylie, 2013) says that "autistic children become aware of their differences when they 'stand out and are unable to fit in' *unless* 'they learn to act or use superficial social skills learned by copying others.' In most cases, children on the spectrum would have sensed their differences by their teenage years."

The following table shows that inevitably there is always a delay between onset of autism (between conception and birth), and when the child receives meaningful support, which may never happen.

The key difference between the second and third degrees of autism is determined by the autistic individual's environment. During the second degree of autism, the individual does not suffer any form of abuse or perceive his or her autistic traits negatively; instead, the individual recognizes that he or she is different without self-judgment or emotional attachment. During the third degree of autism the individual suffers due to his or her difficulties, which may cause secondary psychiatric disorders and mental illness.

Age of occurrence of autism	Between conception and birth
Age of onset (when parents notice the child's differences)	Typically between the ages of 1 and 3
Age of child when he or she becomes aware that he or she is different (without understanding why)	Typically between the ages of 4 and 16
Age of the earlier self-identification and diagnosis (when the individual understands his or her condition)	Typically between 8 and 60, or never
Age when the individual accesses meaningful support	Anytime after diagnosis, or never, because support is usually conditional upon diagnosis

Personal stories

Christa Sorrell (personal correspondence, 2013) had a similar experience of second degree autism, to Philip:

As a young child, I didn't feel any different. I was me and I wanted to be with my Mum. It was all perfectly natural to me, even eating lip salve at Junior School to be ill so I could get home was 'normal' in my eyes. I knew I was bullied but didn't think it was for any specific reason. I did feel 'on the fringe' at secondary school, made worse by it being an all girl's school. I didn't understand the 'ins-and-outs' of fashion, pop idols and so on, which consumed so much of the other girls' time. There were a couple of us misfits and by the age of 16, I realised I really didn't fit in but didn't know why. It was at college, I noticed a real difference but put it down to discovering I was far more intelligent than the average teenager. I also had a difficult home life at the time as my Mum was dying of cancer.

Australian psychologist Dr. Wenn Lawson says he was 13 years old when he began to feel different.

I was probably 13-ish because I kept thinking that it's everybody else who's different, and waiting for them to be more normal really because their interests, their conversational style, the way they related to each other just seemed really odd. Then, it occurred to me that there are more people like them and less people like me, and therefore that makes me the odd one, not them. I would have been 13-ish then.

Danny Beath says:

I have always known I was different from childhood, when I was bullied at school for being 'strange'. I learned from an early age just how intolerant other children are and how quickly they can make judgments. As a kid, I exhibited patience and highly tuned observation skills and I was a very shy and quiet individual, something almost unknown in an average noisy and impatient child.

Parents

Some parents are sadly in denial; some are fearful of accepting a diagnosis or of seeking one and some are unsure how to approach the subject with their children. Also, some parents are afraid to approach the subject with their children as they may be unsure of the (parent-perceived) consequences of the child's response to the parents and their own self-concept (child).

Parent observations

Many parents (sometimes via hindsight) notice their baby's difference to other children right from the start.

Some parents can observe such differences, realizing something is twigging their subconscious from the child's birth to roughly the age of 2 or 3, or a bit beyond this age.

Some parents notice significant "changes" in the child's behaviors at specific points in the child's early life (e.g., age 18 months, 2 years, and so on). The point from which parents notice a difference in their child can vary to the next family and individual. Parents often compare "notes" on their observations of their own children. Such information sharing can be cathartic for some parents, in that they may offer or receive support from each other.

Late onset

There may be a late onset or very late labeling of autism in an individual's life. The term "late onset" may also be applied to a child at the time the individual receives a formal recognition of autism. Sometimes prior to such, the parents have been (or again, with hindsight at that point) very aware of some differences. Sometimes at this point – age-defined "late onset" – is when autism spectrum associated behaviors become or emerge as very apparent when one is considered to be entering or has attained an adult age.

The child identifies it

Louise Page (this author) feels that this consideration is very much determined by the child's own developmental stage of self-awareness. The ability to understand such a concept of difference is related to possibly being on the autism spectrum.

Intuitively and what Louise Page believes emanates from a "primal" level, the child may, by degrees, become more aware as time goes on. They are aware of feeling or being treated as different to or by their peers. "Some parents would rather sacrifice the wellbeing of their own child because they fear they would be judged harshly by the community and they are sensitive towards being blamed," says Rod Morris (2014).

Irene Jenks (personal correspondence, April 21, 2014) says:

My son first asked "Why am I so different from everyone else?" when he was twenty-one. At that time I didn't know the answer. I told him it seemed like he was born that way. He was born in 1986, long before most doctors and teachers knew anything about autism. No one ever suggested to me that he be evaluated by a psychologist. It didn't occur to me that there was an explanation for his difference other than that he was my son and my father's grandson and my brother's nephew. Now I believe we are clearly all on the autism spectrum. I was very tuned in to my son's needs and found ways to accommodate them. I am torn as to whether or not either he or I would have been better off knowing that we were autistic as a child or teenager. Mostly I think it would have helped us a lot to understand who we were before attempting college. Neither of us completed college.

The path from second to third degree autism

Theoretically, it could be possible for an autistic person to live most of his or her natural life at the stage of second degree autism. The prerequisite is a favorable environment, which allows individuals to express their self authentically and to pursue their special interests without restriction. Ideally, their carers would be extremely empathetic and patient, and they would live in a community with either other autistic people or empathetic, caring neuro-typical people. Few autistic people live in such a favorable environment. Also, it could be argued that passing from second degree autism into third degree autism is a right of passage that, although incorporating pain and discomfort, makes us stronger once we embrace the real self of who we are.

References

Happe, F., & Frith, U. (1995). Theory of mind in autism. In E. Schopler, and G. B. Mesibov (Eds.), *Learning and cognition in autism* (pp. 177–197). New York: Plenum Press.

Morris, R. (2014). Master's Thesis. Sheffield Hallam University, Sheffield, UK.

5

The third degree of autism
Developing secondary health issues

Laura Battles

> And so it was that with much ado I was corrupted and made to learn the dirty devices of the world.
> "Centuries of Meditations" by Thomas Traherne (1636–1674)

Introduction

The social constructs that are taught and learned by those who function within a Neuro Typical (NT) state are built on the essentiality of normalization and conformity. The following of social rules allows passage to a society where endemic homogenization forms an infrastructure from childhood to adulthood; where being the same is ranked above diversity and uniqueness. However, children are not born conformist. Instead, they are environmentally shaped and conditioned to follow a social and cultural path leading to the graduation of a "normally" functioning being.

It is this corruption of the formative mind that leads to the scaffolding of power among the majority and the isolation and ostracization of the few. Has this learned behavior developed as a progressive process of selection? Or is it the early years catalyst for man's blind indifference to his fellow man? The social conditioning framework within the institution that is school, the normative shaping of cultural procedures by the media, and the tactical social calculations for the growth of social capital allow the exercise of a complex form of power with the majority of the population as its target. Principally, this forms a social, political, and financial economy with its essential technical apparatus being security and sanitization.

> < + or – Deviant behavior away from?

The deviant development away from normative milestones can impact on both the conscious and the subconscious mind within the forming brain of the child. For example, the range of sensory issues that first emerge in the autistic infant can, if not identified or understood, form developmental anxiety and fear. For example, the autistic child who is sensitive to food textures and tastes may appear to the parent to be a fussy eater particularly when the food is deemed by the manufacturer to mothers as full of healthy vitamins and minerals. There are adverts of plump babies devouring the baby food while mum happily smiles at her splendid child. These are far removed from the screaming, gagging baby with autism and the exhausted mum concerned for her child's well-being.

At this stage in a child's development it is rare that autism is diagnosed and of course fussy eating is not necessarily an autistic trait. But the impact on the autistic child as a consequence of a lack of understanding about this sensory issue can be significant and long lasting. As a result the development of food fears and anxiety within social eating situations can form an opportunity for both self-induced and socially directed isolation. However, if the developing child, and caregiver, even without a diagnosis of autism, are supported to develop the capability and capacity to understand and manage the sensory processing difference, then there is less likelihood of a negative outcome.

Hypothesis for third degree autism

The key difference between the second and third degrees of autism is that the individual does not suffer initially at the second degree stage; but later adverse environmental factors cause suffering at the third degree stage. Typically, the individual would be a target of abuse and he or she would struggle to cope with normal social conventions. Naturally, third degree autistics would be misunderstood often and unable to access meaningful support.

Within the mainstream preschool setting children are expected to have reached a certain number of developmental milestones at specific chronological ages. Not meeting these milestones provides "red flag indicators" for teachers, parents, and pediatricians. The ability to communicate, interact socially, have developed independence, and exhibit the appropriate stage of play indicate that the child falls within the = (equals) to others domain. However, when red flags are raised a number of outcomes may result:

1. The parent is made aware by teachers that the child is not = to others within the class. The parent becomes anxious.
2. The child is singled out for more attention in order that he or she comes more = to his or her peers. The child becomes anxious.
3. The parent is singled out for not providing the child with the key tools for gaining = status. The parent becomes guilty.
4. The child is left to his or her own devices and grows more isolated as a result. This process is typical of many situations parents and children with autism find themselves in. It is rare that a fifth outcome would result.
5. The parent and child are given the correct support to ensure the child is being taught in a manner appropriate to his or her understanding of the world and that the child is made to feel secure.

In order for the fifth outcome to result less of a focus is required on = to and more attention given to understanding multiple (x) normalities. However, lack of understanding of the true nature of autism at this stage often progresses the transition from the second degree of autism where there is an awareness of difference with little adversity, to the third degree of autism where the society attempts to painfully sculpt away differences and demand conformity.

Transitioning

When the person on the autism spectrum attains the third degree of autism, he or she experiences difficulties without understanding why. This is an extremely confusing state for the individual who is aware that he or she is different, but has not identified the condition and therefore is unable to understand the way he or she feels.

Without self-identification of the neurological condition, the individual is likely to experience many problems in life, especially in relationships. The longer the delay between second degree autism and self-identification (at the fourth degree of autism), the more painful the suffering would be. Luke Beardon reminds us it's important to note not all individuals will experience mental health issues. Some may skip from second degree to fourth degree autism without ever going through third degree autism.

Vulnerability to abuse

Many people with autism find themselves in situations where they are catapulted from a state of being born with autism, an alternative normality, to having to cope with living with autism in a singularly normative world. This journey is fraught with obstacles, real and perceived dangers, where people's actions and intentions become more and more disconjugated and the need for safe, alternative cognitive mind spaces is required to be developed. Lack of understanding of alternative normality can lead to people with autism being heinously abused in society.

Autistic people are vulnerable to abuse by predators and other people who lack affective empathy. This is particularly challenging for individuals who have not identified their condition because they would not be fully aware of their strengths and weaknesses.

Some autistic individuals may have limited Theory of Mind (or cognitive empathy). Therefore, they will have difficulty perceiving other people's agendas, unspoken thoughts, and unexpressed feelings. Unfortunately, abusers target vulnerable people who have disabilities, and autistic people can naively trust them, making them easy targets for bullying or deception.

Although some autistic people have difficulties with Theory of Mind, many tend to be extremely compassionate toward anyone who suffers, including underdogs and scapegoats. This means that people who are on the autism spectrum tend to have more affective empathy than many other typical people realize.

Abusers, on the other hand, have adept Theory of Mind but lack Affective empathy. This means that abusers have the ability to perceive other people's thoughts and feelings, but they actually enjoy witnessing the suffering of others. Therefore, abusers have a cruel disposition and ability to identify vulnerable targets, especially people who are on the autism spectrum.

For many people with autism school opens the way for abuse to commence. Alternative normality is rarely welcomed, as the controlled manufacturing of pupils is key to the success of league table outcomes. Children are shaped to be the way society needs them to be. They are taught social rules and are praised for following them. They learn a curriculum of prescribed academics and get certified for their achievements. They learn about knowledge and power. They make friends and gain the ability to read between the lines. The child with autism often struggles with all of the above and the lack of understanding of teachers and pupils means that the child's own identity can become scarred and malformed. Social abuse is widespread and inherent in many schools and the notion of social control, academic gain, and cultural conformity leaves those standing outside of the box in an institutional no man's land.

Environmental factors

Adverse environmental factors do not cause autism but they cause individuals on the autism spectrum to suffer in many ways.

The autistic individual suffers from the third degree of autism through to the sixth degree of autism, until he or she has fully accepted the authentic self. However, during identity alignment, the individual has the added issue of reconstructing his or her self-identity, which may cause the individual to lose confidence in himself or herself.

Funding on research into how environmental factors affect autistic people is minimal. Rod Morris (personal correspondence, 2013) claims that just 1% of paid research covers the effect of environment on people who have neurological conditions.

The main adverse environmental factors that affect people on the autism spectrum are:

• Traumatic brain injury at birth
• Ridicule, teasing, and bullying
• Being treated as inferior within the family
• Misdiagnosis and mistreatment
• Discrimination in the workforce
• Exclusion from society

Affect on self-esteem

Sara Heath mentions that, "Intimidation or rejection happens as other typical children develop an ability to pick out the children who do not fit and then either bully or ostracize them. This then makes Aspie kids who are already anxious, even more socially anxious – so they fail and are bullied or rejected even more" (personal correspondence, 2013).

Rod Morris comments, "An integral part of a child's development is having a firm grasp of their identity. Confident children have a firm understanding of who they are" (personal correspondence, 2013). It follows, therefore, that children who are bewildered by their perceived differences relative to their peers would develop low self-esteem among other personality issues.

Many people with autism who are undiagnosed particularly in early teenage years can develop a significant sense of self-loathing, anger, and frustration in relation to the expectations placed on them. The task of waking in the morning to face a world where your presence is abhorred because other people fail to comprehend or accept that an individual may see, feel, and experience the world differently can slowly erode like a cancer any sense of belonging and meaning. In schools, many of these children take refuge away from their peers outside of class in the far reaches of a corridor armed with earphones and loud music to ameliorate their sense of social solitude. Being made a social outcast in an environment where being able to read between the lines of people's behavior provides the currency for acceptability can brutally incarcerate the character of a child, leaving only a shadow and a desire to be invisible.

Unfortunately, many autistic individuals live most of their lives stuck at the third degree of autism. This means that they never fully understood who they are.

Definition of late diagnosis

The definition of "late diagnosis" concerns the length of time the individual lives at the third degree of autism. Essentially, this developmental stage is one of immense suffering because the individual has developed a false self-identity and is not equipped to protect himself or herself from negative environmental factors.

This false self-identity may develop from a sense of self-guilt or self-loathing from exposure to social alienation and the suppression, silencing, or trampling of the growth of the true character. The damage that can be inflicted on an individual who has been subjected to such abuse can cause a slippage between the individual's perspective of that which is reasonable and that which is rational resulting in a marginalized perception of both the world and the individual's self in it. This can unfortunately lead to further social rejection with the mask required to try to pretend to be normal becoming visible, leaving the individual disarmed and vulnerable.

Late diagnosis occurs if the person with autism develops secondary psychiatric issues or mental health issues. In other words, late diagnosis is evident when the individual experiences other health issues due to non-self-identification and the negative environmental factors.

By definition, every individual who experiences third degree autism, and therefore develops secondary mental health issues, falls under the term "late diagnosis." The degree of lateness, or delay in self-identification, relates proportionally to the damage caused by adverse environmental factors.

Secondary health issues

Many third degree individuals with autism develop secondary health issues unless they are protected in a caring environment.

The most common mental health issues resulting from third degree autism are:

• Depression
• Anxiety
• Insomnia
• Stress

These mental health issues are often not developed in isolation from each other and can present within a person in combination. Recognition of the health issues is often dependent on others recognizing changes in presentation or heightening of behaviors within typical presentation. The success of treatment is dependent on the knowledge and experience of practitioners, which unfortunately is often poor and inadequate, leading to inappropriate treatment further exacerbating health. A chemical cosh can cause further indignity and damage if not given alongside a genuine willingness by medical practitioners to listen, observe, open their minds, and learn.

Coping strategies

Tony Attwood (Attwood, 2007) cites four main coping strategies for individuals who are on the autism spectrum and who experience negative environmental factors. They are:

- Retreat into the realm of imagination or fantasy, in a world where they can be more successful
- Withdrawal and use of drugs or alcohol to annul the pain
- Blaming others for their difficulties
- Copying others (or pretending to be normal) as a survival strategy

NT's may perceive withdrawal into the realm of fantasy or imagination as madness. However, this strategy is simply a way of avoiding an unbearable reality, which causes immense suffering. Virtual reality has a level of control that allows an individual to live safely in a world where differences are recognized as virtues and characteristics that are unique are celebrated. There is also the ability to pause the world in order to take stock. Indeed, people with autism can, with the stratagem of fantasy worlds and imagination, develop a sense of disrobing from the shackles of pretense and allowing space to breathe. This retreat is neither profanation nor extravagance, but a self-serving moral and ethical journey to ensure personal objectivity and reason are maintained, albeit temporarily.

Use of alcohol or other drugs may relieve the individual's suffering for a temporary period. However, continued use without the correct support can often lead to addiction, which is a physical and spiritual disease. Many people who are on the autism spectrum find themselves distrustful of psychiatric drugs, which often have counterproductive side effects where feelings are numbed and dulled and the sound of white noise and static dominates, masking a tinnitus of misunderstanding.

Blaming others for the difficulties endured is common and without the correct response and support can lead to the manifestation of internal and external counter natural bellicosity.

Pretending to be normal (or wearing masks) by mimicking other people's actions is a highly effective strategy for accessing and maintaining societal acceptance, but it takes its toll on the individual's mental health. The behavior is not authentic so the individual is not being his or her true self. It can lead to both mental and physical exhaustion and further embedment of destructed self-worth. Pretending to be normal is particularly prevalent in girls, which may be an indicator why many girls are diagnosed late.

In addition, the medical model of autism is aligned with Cognitive Behavioral Therapy (CBT), which influences neurologically diverse individuals to act as Neuro Typical (NT) people do. CBT treats people as "cured" when their behavior is outwardly normal. However, this model is flawed because it can cause internal conflict and can have a devastating affect on the individual's self-esteem.

Chronology

While the majority of people who are on the autism spectrum begin to be aware of their "different" traits around the age of 12, there is a wide spread of ages where neurological conditions are recognized or acknowledged.

The third degree individuals who identify themselves during their teens may be considered late-diagnosed, but those who identify themselves after the age of 20 should be counted as "extremely late diagnosed."

> A late diagnosis is when a person has developed a profile of wrong perspectives and wrong explanations so that the person's perspective of 'themselves' are totally false. This can cause a great deal of fallout, grief not to mention a very severe identity crisis once the diagnosis has been made.
>
> (Rod Wintour, personal correspondence, 2014)

When that diagnosis comes in later life many of the perspectives mentioned above have become so interwoven within the person's own structure that the person is unable to pull apart the pretense and the reality.

Tragically, there are a significant number of individuals out there who have never been diagnosed and they are baffled about themselves. They can be misdiagnosed as Schizophrenic or having Borderline Personality Disorder or Personality Disorder. Misdiagnosis of Asperger's syndrome is a huge issue in adult psychiatry. Anxiety Disorder may also be diagnosed in adults, but often the underlying Asperger's syndrome is missed. There are several other possible reasons for this:

- Denial: the person will not seek diagnosis as he or she may be fearful or stuck in a spiral of pretense and reality.
- Living within a supportive and protected environment.
- Missing childhood screening where red flags may be indicated.

The path from third to fourth degree autism

The path from the third degree to the fourth degree of autism involves self-identification, which may be followed by an official diagnosis. The two most common pathways for self-identification are other autistic relatives who receive a diagnosis and media coverage, typically articles about Asperger's syndrome or autism in magazines, newspapers, or television programs, radio talk shows, or comments posted on the Internet.

However, the journey from third to fourth degree autism is unique to each individual and, depending on the support systems that are available, can be a very lonely path to travel. Having mentally shifted from an unconscious not knowing to a conscious knowing that there are both internal and external differences between the person with autism and his or her NT peers can cause significant challenge and pain. For some, the problems that come with not fitting in and having little or no support to understand why can cause irreversible damage that remains even when a diagnosis is given. The protective felt suit adorned daily, required as a form of self-defense, continues to weigh heavy.

Conclusion

The means to diagnosis may come about in several ways: as a result of parental or self-study, identification of similarities to other family members or peers who exhibit similar traits, television and media coverage on the subject, or as a result of a breakdown leading to investigation regarding cause. However, for many the journey will not end at diagnosis as this often raises more questions than it resolves and the support provided to journey on often determines the person's ability to accept and establish a positive sense of self.

References

Attwood, T. (2007). *The complete guide to Asperger's syndrome*. London: Jessica Kingsley Publishers.

Medical News Today. Retrieved from http://www.medicalnewstoday.com/articles/192361.php

6

The fourth degree of autism

Self-identification

Debra Moore

Introduction

The fourth degree of autism begins with an awareness of oneself as possibly being autistic. You may have a sudden shock of recognition – often after reading or hearing a description of typical traits associated with Asperger's syndrome (AS) or autism. Or your awareness may emerge hesitantly, with repeated cycles of curiosity-identification-repudiation, as you struggle to integrate information that requires a fundamental shift in self-perception.

For many people, a curious intellect and comfort with the Internet naturally lead to online research on medical and psychological sites, as well as a survey of personal memoirs, blogs, and autism communities. You may discover a newfound sense of having found "a home," yet initially you may also experience a tangled mix of reactions. The intensity of this first flood of information, emotions, and altered perceptions can be overwhelming and you may understandably retreat for a time.

Whether weeks or years later, you will likely come to recognize that you have persisting questions and that you want more detailed information. Having lived with a sense of not fitting in for so long, you may be hungry for validation that you've finally found a place of refuge. At this point you may turn to a current physician or counselor for a formal diagnosis or seek out an expert in autism for a comprehensive evaluation.

The hypothesis for this model

The journey from birth on the autism spectrum to self-awareness, acceptance, and knowledge can reach past childhood into adolescence and adulthood. For many on the spectrum, there are predictable stages to this odyssey. A person progressing through these levels or degrees of awareness may find it valuable to seek input from others, including professionals.

While it is possible for an autistic person to progress to ninth degree autism without receiving a formal diagnosis or other professional opinion, foregoing this step has important drawbacks. Incorrect self-diagnosis can prevent recognition and handling of other conditions that may better account for your identification with autistic traits. Also, self-identification in the absence of professional consultation generally limits exposure to the full range of available support and resources. Finally, a professional consultation and diagnosis often includes information for significant others – including partners, family, friends, and employers.

An identity crisis often characterizes the fourth degree of autism, which continues through to self-acceptance at the seventh degree. This experience can be devastating without adequate information and support. The severity of the crisis depends on several factors, including the age at which the self-identification occurs, whether appropriate mental health support services are available, and how employers, friends, and family react.

Successful self-identification gradually evolves from initial disequilibrium to a newly formed and eventually solidified and accurate self-perception. Old memories and experiences are now filtered through a clearer lens, and your life story emerges with more clarity as previously confusing experiences begin to make sense.

As you deconstruct your old self-image and reconstruct a new self-identity, you may shift perspective on long-held values and beliefs. Tony Attwood points out that self-identification later in life can also help create a future focus on strengths rather than trying to resolve weaknesses (Attwood, 2013). You potentially embark on the beginning of a new life!

Pathways to self-identification

Awareness of AS and autism has risen dramatically within the past decade. The majority of the research, however, has focused on children. Much of what we know about adults with autism comes from those who have self-identified or been professionally evaluated. As a "hardwired" developmental difference, autism is by definition present throughout the life span. While compensatory behaviors may develop over time, the basic differences in information processing, communication, and sensory sensitivity remain present. Thus, we would expect that the prevalence rate of autism remains consistent across childhood and adolescence and then into adulthood.

Most recent epidemiological studies cite a prevalence rate of autism spectrum disorders in children between 2% and 5%. Approximately one in 42 boys and one in 189 girls meet the diagnostic criteria (Baio, 2014). A 2009 UK study found that for every three cases of an autism condition that are now diagnosed in children of primary-school age, two more cases go undetected (Baron-Cohen et al., 2009). Considering that this study was conducted only a few years ago, the rate of undiagnosed persons now in their middle or later adult years can reasonably be hypothesized as many times higher.

There seem to be three main pathways by which autism appears on the radar of adults in today's world, thus beginning the shift from third degree autism to fourth degree autism. The most common is a chance encounter with a description of autism traits in the media. Many popular television programs have featured either real-life profiles or fictional depictions of someone with Asperger's or autism. Popular magazines as well as newspapers have increasingly published research findings and personal accounts. Several widely distributed movies have been released with Asperger's syndrome prominently featured in their publicity and marketing materials.

The second typical route to self-diagnosis is having your child diagnosed and realizing that the evaluator's description of autism in fact fits you. Sometimes this awareness comes quickly, and other times it dawns during subsequent visits with a counselor. Your partner may recognize the similarities before you do.

A third road to diagnosis begins with a counselor questioning whether your mental health concerns such as depression, anxiety, or social challenges could be at least partially accounted for by autism. While physicians are often unfamiliar with Asperger's syndrome or autism, increasing numbers of psychologists, psychiatrists, and neurologists have at least some understanding of autism spectrum challenges. Those trained after 1994, the year that Asperger's syndrome was included in the formal diagnostic nomenclature of the American Psychiatric Association, are more equipped to recognize nuanced traits and patterns that may be mistaken for other psychological conditions such as mood or personality disorders.

Other possible triggers for self-diagnosis include crises in vocational, family, or personal life. Many intellectually high-functioning people with autism have developed sophisticated ways to adapt to their environment. These compensatory strategies often work up to a point and then eventually fail during developmental transitions that demand greater levels of complexity.

Examples of triggers include many "firsts" such as transitions out of a parental home, entering or ending a relationship, starting a job, having a child, or retiring. Crises can also arise when environments require adaptation to new structure or routine. Moving, getting a new work supervisor, being asked to step into a management role, or needing to adapt to illness in oneself or a family member can overwhelm due to anxiety triggered by unpredictable change.

Informal first steps

Learning more after our initial exposure to autism is relatively easy due to the wealth of online information that is currently available. Entire communities such as wrongplanet.net have now existed for the past decade. Many Internet sites include informal "quizzes" for self-diagnosis. Thus begins a journey of self-discovery!

There are numerous benefits to taking online screenings. At this stage in self-identification, some degree of ambivalence or even denial usually persists. Reading multiple statements that fit uncannily well with your experience can help you become more open to the possibility that Asperger's has played a significant role in your life. Questions may cover areas of your personal history that you would never have realized are related to being on the autism spectrum. Your self-understanding begins to broaden.

Online screenings also have several drawbacks. They rely on self-observation and are subject to your blind spots. Few of these assessments have been tested on large sample sizes, so their statistical reliability or validity may be questionable. Most important, online screenings do not differentiate between autism and other conditions. For example, you may agree with the statement "I have difficulty in social situations," but this might also be endorsed by someone not on the autism spectrum but who is challenged by generalized anxiety, depression, or social phobia.

Popular online self-screening instruments

Asperger's Quotient Test (AQ Test)
This questionnaire gives the option of "definitely" or "slightly" agreeing or disagreeing with 50 statements assessing areas of social skill, attention switching, attention to detail, communication, and imagination. Developed in 2001 by psychologist Simon Baron-Cohen and colleagues at Cambridge's Autism Research Centre, this popular instrument is even available as an iPhone app. Of those who have been diagnosed with autism or Asperger's, 80% score 32 or higher, compared to only 2% of the control group.

Adult Asperger's Assessment (AAA)
Also developed by Simon Baron-Cohen and colleagues (2005), this test is modeled on the diagnostic criteria from the *DSM-IV*. It conservatively includes additional questions to prevent false positive results. Respondents are simply asked if they agree or disagree with descriptive statements.

Empathy Quotient (EQ)
Simon Baron-Cohen and colleagues (2004) designed this 60-item questionnaire to specifically measure the ability to empathize. The measure uses 40 questions assessing empathy plus 20 filler questions. Of those diagnosed with autism or Asperger's, 80% of adults score less than 80, compared to only 10% of controls.

The Aspie Quiz (rdos.net/end/Aspie-quiz)
Developed by a Swedish systems programmer, Leif Ekblad, this popular online quiz has undergone revisions over the years. Developed from the perspective of assessing neurodiverse traits, this computer-scored test will give you a report and presents results graphically. While it doesn't come with academic credentials and should not be used diagnostically, you may learn about your patterns in areas typically affected by Asperger's.

The Ritvo Autism Asperger's Diagnostic Scale (RAADS)
This test was developed in 2008 and revised in 2010. Its 80 questions measure the areas of social relatedness, circumscribed interests, language, and sensory motor functioning.

No single test can substitute for a comprehensive evaluation. While they are often a valuable step on the journey of self-identification, online self-screening instruments are best used as a source of preliminary data.

Weighing the option of a formal diagnosis

When you reach a "tipping point" in your search, and have accumulated enough information to realize that autism seems to be a reasonable explanation for many of your life experiences, you'll likely want the confirmation from a professional diagnostic evaluation. Even so, you may continue to go "back and forth" about this next step. Some days it makes perfect logical sense – after all, data is good, right? Other days, it appears a waste of time and funds.

Your task is to figure out whether hesitation about a professional evaluation is logical or primarily fear-based. If you are hesitant about seeking a formal diagnostic evaluation, these questions may help sort it out:

1. Do I worry what others would think if it turns out I am diagnosed with autism?
2. Are there specific people in my life I would not want to know? Why?
3. Do I think I would be somehow "inferior" or "defective" if I get a diagnosis?
4. Have I had negative experiences with mental health evaluators or therapists?
5. Do I distrust professionals in general and fear they don't know what they are doing?
6. Do I hate opening up and talking about myself? Am I afraid what an evaluator might ask?

Answering "yes" to many of these questions is not surprising. Most people remain quite ignorant about autism and negative stereotypes and misunderstandings abound. A bit of caution is realistic.

You may understandably be concerned about the reaction of others in your life. Others may be uninformed and thus minimize or discount entirely the whole idea of autism. If you tried before to bring up the subject and had it rejected, your feelings are probably hurt and you naturally feel anxious about revisiting the topic.

What about your own stereotypes and judgments? If you've gone your entire life thinking you are different from others, and in fact have been treated as an outcast or "less than," it is likely you have at least partially internalized these ideas.

Many people with undiagnosed autism have had previous experiences with mental health counselors or psychiatrists, and often these encounters were more frustrating than helpful. You may have been given one or more psychological diagnoses over the years. These diagnoses may have been given with what seemed like complete confidence on the part of the professional, and yet you never felt like they really fit. But perhaps you told yourself the professionals "must know what they're talking about."

The fact is that characteristics of autism have only recently been fully described and taught, even to specialists in psychology and psychiatry. If you saw a mental health professional as a child, or even just a decade ago, the odds are that they were completely unfamiliar with AS! As a result, many people with undiagnosed autism have been misdiagnosed and received treatments that were useless or even harmful.

Fortunately, more recently graduated professionals have had at least some exposure to autism – hopefully enough to recognize when to make a referral to a specialist if they have not received targeted training in this area.

Perhaps you distrust professionals in general. If you went through school feeling smarter than most of your peers (which you well may have been), you may have developed the dangerous habit of assuming everyone around you is "stupid." If, as a child, you even thought you were smarter than your teachers (after all, if the subject happened to be an interest of yours, you probably did know tons more than the instructor!), you've most likely generalized this distrust to most "authorities."

It may be helpful to recognize this tendency and to remind yourself that legitimate professionals in the area of autism have been steeped in more information than you've likely had access to. Even if you've read voraciously, you are likely uninformed about related diagnoses and comorbid conditions that may require ruling out. These might be a great number of disorders including those related to mood, thought processes, sensory processing, learning, or personality. Experienced clinicians will also explore whether past trauma is impacting you.

It is also likely that your exposure to others with autism has been limited. Experienced evaluators have conducted enough assessments to recognize a wide range of autism concerns and presentations. They are able to identify the many and often subtle manifestations of autism.

You may also avoid an evaluation because you are hesitant about being "scrutinized" or sharing personal information with a stranger. I suppose the question to ask yourself is whether continuing to go through life wondering is a better alternative. That approach is anxiety-provoking as well. It may be more of a chronic, lower-level anxiety, but over a lifetime it adds up. It really is exhausting!

In proceeding with an evaluation it may help to tell yourself that you are simply going to gather data. You are likely to become curious during the evaluation as you join the professional in being a "detective" about yourself. Most people begin an evaluation feeling nervous, but quickly relax and often end up actually enjoying learning more about themselves and autism.

Remember that you are in control during an evaluation. If there are questions you don't want to answer, you can decline. An open mind is helpful, but knowing you also have the right to decide what to share can help you feel more comfortable.

How a diagnosis can help

There are seven significant ways having a professional diagnosis can help you.

1. You will gain a framework that helps you better understand your experiences.
2. You can start to view yourself more realistically and positively.
3. Others in your life can begin to understand you.
4. Diagnosis will guide any future counseling or coaching.
5. A formal diagnosis may help you qualify for academic or workplace accommodations or informal assistance.
6. A formal diagnosis of accompanying impairment may enable you to qualify for disability benefits or vocational training programs. (The diagnosis alone will not usually qualify you. It is generally a specific impairment that is considered disabling or qualifying.)
7. A formal diagnosis can provide protection under other national laws, such as the Equality Act in Great Britain and the Americans with Disabilities Act in the United States.

Most important, we all have a need to make sense of ourselves. In the absence of validated explanations for our feelings or experiences, we make up our own. Most adults with undiagnosed autism started thinking of themselves in certain fixed ways early in life. Even if some of these labels were positive (like "smart," "curious," "brainy"), these terms still implied different. Sadly, though, many times these self-imposed labels were negative and hurtful. Many adults remember thinking, "something is wrong with me" or "I am weird."

Peers and even family members may have reinforced these labels. Research has repeatedly found that a majority of those with an autism condition report being bullied as children or teens. Rates vary widely, from upward of 60% to close to 100% (e.g., Heinrichs & Smith Myles, 2003). Many adults remember abuse even from parents or siblings. Often this took the form of verbal name calling or being teased or taunted. Sometimes it even took the form of being shunned or abusively punished.

If you had recurrent meltdowns as a child, your parents may have became overwhelmed and unable to calm you. Their efforts might well have made things worse. What "worked" with their other children may have backfired with you. These sorts of repeated experiences may have reinforced their own sense of ineptness. With no explanation or framework for understanding, they simply blamed themselves and/or you.

Also teachers often had no idea how to interact with students with autism. Overwhelmed by noisy classrooms, cafeterias, or playgrounds, you probably had little help in handling your discomfort. You may have been forced to endure chronic overstimulation. Ironically, other times you may have been horribly bored – which paradoxically can lead to intense anxiety. Teachers may have told you (or your parents) that you "didn't pay attention" or were "uncooperative" or "defiant." More likely, you were simply frustrated. And worse, you didn't even know why!

Again, without a diagnostic framework to put your varied struggles into, it is likely that you came up with your own labels. Lacking accurate perspective and information, you may have clumsily grouped your various traits into false categories. Without an alternative, you may have placed both erroneous and harsh labels on your "differences." Also, instead of regarding them as just one aspect of your life, those differences may have come to constitute your primary self-definition.

With a diagnostic framework, however, many experiences can now start to make sense. Attributions of blame can begin to shift to important recognition of your struggle and appropriate empathy for your tenaciousness and courage.

It should be noted that a valuable controversy exists over whether autism (and many other psychiatric diagnoses or disabilities) should be labeled. My perspective is that some sort of consensually and agreed-upon framework helps us communicate accurately and efficiently. We need terms that allow us to conceptualize a constellation of characteristics consistently, whether we are selecting participants for research studies or designing effective approaches for helping people.

The social model of autism examines the concept of social oppression as it applies to disabled people and the role of diagnoses or labels in potentially fostering maltreatment. This author believes the point of diagnoses is to gain understanding in order to provide help, reduce marginalization, and increase self-expression. It would be naive, however, to fail to recognize that societies have often persecuted those given labels of "disability." During this process of digesting information about yourself, reading more about the social model is encouraged.

The diagnostic markers of autism are neither "good" nor "bad." They are simply various aspects of how we process information. Each diagnostic criterion can be seen from two perspectives – how it helps and how it hinders. By definition, all *DSM* diagnoses focus on the aspects of a condition that impair the person. This is because the psychiatric profession is attempting to distinguish between the simple presence of traits versus a pervasive and impairing presence. Many medical conditions are diagnosed based on the presence of a distinct marker, such as cancer cells, bacteria, or viruses. In contrast, autism is a spectrum disorder that is identified by a pattern of behavioral characteristics. Tendencies toward these patterns are also often found in people who do not meet diagnostic criteria.

Whether meeting a diagnostic threshold or not, there are often equally strong but overlooked advantages to these tendencies. For example, "restricted, repetitive interests or behaviors" impair a person unless his or her environment calls for just this type of focus. In a "good fit" environment, these qualities may make you the best person for the job! With accurate awareness of your characteristics, you are better prepared to advocate for yourself in all environments.

Understanding how your typical ways of processing information, navigating the world, and expressing yourself are part of the autism "package" will help you put these aspects of yourself in perspective. When people who care about you are also educated, they often come to genuinely appreciate your unique strengths and assets.

Another important reason for obtaining a professional diagnosis is that it may help you get appropriate guidance, coaching, counseling, or other support. Think of it this way: if suddenly one day your computer won't turn on, you need to know the cause. If there is a power cut, that's one thing; however, if the power source is intact, but it's not connecting to your computer, that's a different situation. And if the power and connection are both fine, but the computer is not registering the input, that's yet another issue. Without having an accurate diagnosis you're just guessing at a solution. And odds are you'll end up wasting time and effort and will be frustrated as well.

If you are an adult with autism but without a diagnosis, you are in just this type of situation. Encountering daily challenges in a neuro-typical world, you must strategize ways to maneuver in a "foreign" environment. Unguided by accurate information you most likely make misguided and unsuccessful attempts to navigate. You may have become so frustrated you've basically stopped trying. You may have found yourself left with resentment, exhaustion, or hopelessness.

Mental health professionals are at a serious disadvantage if they do not recognize autism in their client. Like the teacher who believes all students should be able to learn the same way, some therapists uniformly apply treatment methods to all of their clients who act in certain ways, assuming they should all benefit. If your therapist is uninformed about autism, and approaches treatment as though everyone is neuro-typical, your results will suffer. The therapist may even conclude you "weren't really trying" or were "resistant."

A common example is the therapist who focuses on your feelings to the exclusion of your logical thought process. Without helping you step by step through your reactions to a situation, and without realizing how your brain may "freeze" when overly stimulated or pressured, they may simply conclude you lack empathy. But if they understand you are impacted by autism and can thus know to guide you via logical analysis and then incorporate feelings once a situation is broken down into manageable chunks, they will be much more likely to help successfully.

Adults with undiagnosed autism can be quite damaged by traditional couples counseling. If the counselor attributes the communication style of the autistic partner to personality alone and has no insight into the neurological underpinnings, the couple is at a real disadvantage. Not only is the therapy unlikely to be helpful, there is a very real possibility that it will be harmful.

A final primary reason for a professional diagnosis involves gaining access to valuable support, either informally or through an official program. If you are employed in a neuro-typical environment, you've probably encountered at least some challenges unique to having autism. You may have noticed certain tasks or situations are difficult for you but not for your coworkers. If you approach your employer for help, you may have been perceived as too demanding or even unqualified. Yet with some education about autism, a compassionate employer is likely to work together with an employee to achieve good results that benefit both of you.

Sometimes it is necessary to document a diagnosis formally. This is likely to be required for academic institutions if you want special arrangements or accommodations for studying, taking tests, or performing assignments. Many universities have their own set of forms that a professional must complete, documenting both a formal diagnosis and specific needs. Some institutions even have a list of particular assessment measures they require the evaluator to use.

Larger workplaces also tend to have policies and procedures in place for employees with documented "disabilities." If your company has a human resource manager, he or she is probably the best person to consult. Depending on your locale, legislation may exist which determines your rights and what accommodations are mandated. These laws often dictate which allowances can be made to areas such as scheduling, the physical work environment, and how tasks are presented to you.

Special considerations for females seeking a diagnosis

Research on women on the autism spectrum remains limited. Prevalence estimates of Asperger's syndrome in females vary widely. The most oft-cited gender ratio for autism remains 4:1 males to females. For Asperger's, ratios of 14:1 are often quoted, yet other clinicians believe the true proportion is more likely only 2.5:1 (Gould & Ashton

Smith, 2011). While many researchers believe the male genotype supports this imbalance, others are unconvinced.

First, these proportions are based on studies of children, not adults. Due to generally slower developmental trajectories for males, boys struggle more frequently in primary grades. They are more likely to come to the attention of school personnel, resulting in more referrals to specialists and subsequent diagnosis.

Second, expression of autistic characteristics may be quite different in women, who some speculate, respond to gender socialization by higher levels of compensatory social behaviors.

Other researchers speculate that many females go undiagnosed because clinicians misattribute their traits to other disorders, primarily anxiety and depression, and even eating disorders. If a comorbid disorder is perceived as the main reason for a woman's presentation, a professional may prematurely stop there and miss other signs of autism.

Pioneering developmental psychologist Uta Frith remarked,

I wish there was more evidence as to the way autism is expressed in the behavior of females. They can "pass for normal" as we know from the gifted women who lucidly write about their autism.

The distinction between justifiable social anxiety and a social anxiety disorder is important. For many autistic adults, it may be the difference between the road to self-acceptance and reasonable accommodations or years of self-defeating therapy to fix a disorder that doesn't exist.

(Frith, 2013)

Some women have an additional reason for avoiding a diagnosis. Mothers may fear that an authority or a spouse could later use this label as a weapon in a child custody battle. Women often believe that mothers are held to a higher parenting standard than fathers. Combined with difficulty navigating interpersonal conflict and interpreting hidden intent, this creates a reasonable risk factor.

> ### *Hiding in plain sight*
>
> Many women have similar memories of childhood – either of being taught social rules explicitly or of learning to model the social behaviors of peers. Growing into adulthood, we often learn to hide in plain sight, suppressing our more obvious autistic traits while going through our days feeling as if we're faking social interactions.
>
> Often, women seek a diagnosis because they can't escape the feeling that something is fundamentally wrong. Society expects women to have strong intuitive social skills. Many autistic women talk of their belief that one day they would "mature" or simply "get it." When they reach adulthood or midlife and that still hasn't happened, they begin looking for another explanation.
>
> Unfortunately, by that point, many women have become so adept at passing as normal that mental health professionals refuse to believe they're autistic. Some clinicians still hold damaging stereotypes of autism when it comes to women and adults in general. Women who suspect they may be autistic are told by professionals that they simply can't be on the spectrum because they are too social, make eye contact, have a sense of humor, are married, have children, or are empathetic and caring (Kim, 2013).

What is included in a formal diagnosis?

There is a huge difference between a professional's "opinion" and a formal assessment and diagnosis. It is important to consider three variables when proceeding with a diagnostic evaluation.

1. *The purpose of the evaluation.* There are many appropriate reasons for wanting an actual diagnosis and your reason may partially dictate your next steps.
2. *The evaluator and his or her academic/clinical training.* You want an evaluator who has been well trained not just in his or her general field of study (such as psychiatry or psychology) but who has an academic background specializing in autism. The best background combines specialized formal classes, combined with attendance at workshops and conferences, and a habit of reading voraciously on the subject of autism.
3. *The actual hands-on experience of the evaluator.* You want someone who has done many evaluations of both children and adults. All the academic training in the world is not a substitute for clinical practice.

It is perfectly acceptable to ask a potential evaluator about his or her experience level, and it is also recommended that you research the person online and check credentials with the licensing board.

So now you are ready to proceed. Do you want an informal "opinion" of whether you have AS traits? Is this information primarily for your own satisfaction? Or do you need official documentation of a diagnosis based on criteria from the *DSM* (*Diagnostic and Statistical Manual* – the "bible" of mental health professionals and what insurance companies use to determine eligibility for coverage). Will you need a report in order to document the need for college or workplace accommodations?

If you are seeking an evaluation primarily to satisfy your own curiosity, the most basic and least costly approach is simply to meet once with a counselor and have the person "give you an opinion." Most professionals are quite reluctant to do such a cursory "evaluation." Without more detailed assessment, there is a risk of missing a diagnosis in the adult who has learned to modify behavior to hide areas of impairment or in the adult who does not display more commonly recognized struggles. There is also the risk of a false positive diagnosis, which can result when comorbid conditions mimic autistic traits.

An appropriate approach is to view this sort of meeting as a pre-screening only. The problem I have found, however, is no matter how tentatively phrased, if a professional says he or she "thinks" someone is or isn't on the autism spectrum, that person hears an absolute diagnosis and may not seek further assessment. Alternatively, you may hear the word "think" and become even more frustrated when what you want or need is a definitive answer! A complete assessment includes recommendations for appropriate interventions, treatment, or environmental modifications. A one-shot screening cannot provide these important components.

A thorough diagnostic evaluation will likely utilize several important sources of data about you. You may be asked to bring along someone who knew you as a child as well as a current partner, friend, or coworker. They may be asked to complete questionnaires about you independently. The examiner will likely want to meet with you individually as well as observe you in their company.

If academic records are available, including report cards or educational reports, the evaluator may want to review them. A complete developmental history and family history should be obtained if possible.

You will likely complete several questionnaires that assess a wide range of emotions and conditions. Because anxiety, obsessions and compulsions, and depression are commonly found in those with autism, specific questions about these areas will be asked. Studies have found that up to 70% of those diagnosed with autism also experience at least one comorbid psychiatric condition, with depression occurring in 53%, anxiety in 50%, and obsessive-compulsive disorder in 24% (Hofvander et al., 2009).

You may also be asked about unusual perceptions including hallucinations or delusions, as well as any history of aggression or violence. Your pattern of alcohol and/or drug use should be assessed as well, with particular attention to any tendencies you may have developed to self-medicate painful emotions.

Significant medical history may be reviewed and will typically include questions about head injuries, seizures, tics, and other neurological symptoms or trauma. You may be asked to describe your eating behaviors to see if you have developed any ritualized patterns or restrictions. Your sleeping patterns may be assessed, as sleep is commonly disturbed in those diagnosed with autism (Allik, Larsson, & Smedie, 2006). In one study 70 to 90% of those diagnosed with Asperger's syndrome reported frequent insomnia (Tani et al., 2003).

Unusual sensory reactivity (either under- or over-reactivity) is a common source of distress for those with autism. Your evaluation should include questions or tests to measure how you react to a wide range of incoming sensory stimuli, including sound, light, odor, touch, pressure, texture, temperature, and pain. Studies have shown that 45 to 95% of those with an autism diagnosis report sensory challenges (e.g., Crane et al., 2009).

If you have struggled academically or vocationally, you may take tests designed to evaluate your patterns of information processing and your visual, auditory, and working memory. Assessments that rule out specific learning disabilities (e.g., dyslexia, dyscalculia, dysgraphia) may also be given. If you have struggled with sustaining attention or focus, written or computerized tests for ADD/ADHD may be included.

Social struggles, a necessary component for a diagnosis of autism, can arise from diverse origins. Interpersonal challenges can result from neurological wiring that makes it difficult to perceive and respond to social cues. Such challenges can also develop as a result of trauma, family dysfunction, lack of skill, numerous anxiety conditions, and a range of personality features. It is very important to make these distinctions because recommendations for reducing your social discomfort differ based on its source.

A good diagnostician considers more than your stated responses. Your mannerisms, presentation, style of communication, and social interaction during the assessment are all viewed as useful data. Behavioral interaction with others such as accompanying family members or even with clinic staff can yield important information.

An evaluation can take place in one day or it may be spaced out. Spacing out the evaluation allows the examiner to score and review results and base selection of additional tests on these findings. As "clues" emerge the diagnostician can selectively follow them to obtain increasingly detailed data about your individual make-up and struggles.

Thus, it is appropriate to regard a formal diagnostic evaluation as a process with multiple goals. More than a simple "yes' or "no," a thorough evaluation gives you substantial feedback and insight into yourself. With the findings that emerge, you are better prepared to work around challenges; you can develop increased coping skills, and amplify your natural strengths.

Do not expect to be given a diagnosis the same day you are evaluated. Your examiner needs time to score tests and many clinicians will want time to sift through your findings and thoughtfully consider numerous possible explanations for the patterns that emerge from them.

You will most likely want a written report of the findings. I prefer to have clients review my draft copy via email before I write the final report so that any errors I made in relating their history or concerns are spotted. (I am always amazed at the number of mistakes in reports I review, so I'd prefer to have a spot checker – and what better person than someone with autistic characteristics!)

Schedule plenty of time for a feedback session and come prepared with your questions. You may want to bring someone with you to take notes. The feedback session is a time for you to understand how the diagnosis was arrived at and what it was based on. You will want to take a signed copy of the report home with you.

Thoughts on self-disclosure

This is a sensitive, personal choice that may change over time and across environments. It is important to think carefully about your goals in disclosing instead of impulsively sharing this personal information. You are under no obligation to tell others, even prospective employers. The bottom line is, "it depends."

On the other hand, there are often substantial benefits when others have a fresh context for understanding your reactions and behaviors. For example, they are less likely to be offended, or take minor social missteps in your relationship personally.

Many people decide to share on an "as needed" basis only. That is, instead of a decision to disclose globally, information is given only when it may be expected to improve a relationship or result in appropriate assistance.

If you are in an intimate or committed relationship, you will likely consider at least disclosure to your partner. It is possible that your significant other has already wondered if you were on the autism spectrum but was reluctant to bring up the topic. Being told someone suspected but never discussed it can be quite unsettling. No one likes to think others have insight into us that we ourselves are blind to.

It is difficult to predict the impact of diagnosis and disclosure on an intimate relationship. I have counseled couples that benefited greatly from the enhanced awareness that followed disclosure. In these relationships, struggles were subsequently viewed with more compassion and understanding. Your behaviors that may have previously been interpreted as a personal affront, or a sign of not caring, may now appear as simply a logical consequence of how you process information and handle intimacy.

On the other hand, diagnosis and disclosure was the death knell for some couples I have worked with. I suspect the non-autistic partner in these relationships had little hope left to begin with. Knowing their partner was on the autistic spectrum was interpreted as a sign that nothing would change in the relationship's future. They did not have the energy or commitment to stay and find out.

If your self-identification was triggered by the diagnosis of your child, keep in mind that your partner is already handling a lot. You are both processing a new perspective on your family and the implications of your own diagnosis will become clear over time. You may need to focus primarily on your child for now even if that does not seem fair. Family counseling sessions during this period can be very helpful in facilitating good communication.

In most cases, I have found that disclosure within a friendship is ultimately well received and beneficial. Initially, however, some misperceptions may need to be cleared up. The diagnosis will make perfect sense to some of your friends. *"Well that explains things!"* Others will struggle to integrate your compensatory presentation with a "disability" label. *"But you do just fine!"* They have no appreciation for how exhausted you are at the end of every day from the effort of appearing "fine" while you navigate the neuro-typical world.

Disclosure to family members can result in a wide variety of responses, partially depending on the person's relationship to you. Your siblings, or your older or adult children, may be relieved, thinking you now make "more sense" to them. Some parents (particularly mothers, in my experience) feel guilty for not better recognizing your needs while you were growing up.

The guilt may be accompanied by fear for your future now that you are "disabled" (no matter that nothing has changed and you're still the same person!). If you depend on your parents for housing or financial backing, they may worry about how you will cope once they are gone. Again, while nothing has changed in terms of your abilities, an actual diagnosis may "wake them up" to a more realistic appreciation of your current and future needs. This is likely a good thing and now you can begin to have an open conversation about your future.

For parents unable to tolerate feelings of fear and/or guilt (which may not even be conscious), a phenomenon of projection may occur. Instead of acknowledging their own internal discomfort, they project blame onto you. This can take the form of accusing you of using your diagnosis as an excuse or claiming that you are exaggerating your challenges.

My dad told me quite openly that he didn't want me to have the label of "Asperger Syndrome" because I would use it as an excuse not to tidy my house. This quite bewildered me; I replied to him "Dad, in all these years that I haven't had a diagnosis, my house has always been untidy. So, even if I did use it as an excuse, how is my label of Asperger Syndrome going to change anything?"

(Aspects of Aspergers, 2010)

Finally, other parents may need to completely disavow your diagnosis because they unconsciously recognize the same traits in themselves. If they are not prepared to look within, it is unlikely they will be able to support you in your journey of self-identification. But if they are conscious and accepting of their similarities to you, and are also aware of the genetics of autism, they may eventually embark on their own journey of self-identification.

Self-disclosure sometimes has a larger domino effect, as extended family members begin to explore the possibility that they too are on the spectrum. Your traits and ways of navigating the world may remind them of other relatives, often children who are just beginning to show typical autistic patterns. Your disclosure may be a precious gift. It could be the first step in saving another young family member from enduring the same degree of struggle you experienced.

The pros and cons of disclosure are also important to consider in academic and vocational settings. I have found that in both arenas, the most important determinant of a party's reaction is how much that person knows about autism. Therefore, I advise you to assume they know nothing. Instead of simply sharing your diagnosis, be prepared to outline a general overview of autism as well as specific ways it manifests in you. A brief, bulleted letter has worked very well for many of my clients.

For example, one adult I worked with was planning to apply to a competitive graduate program. He struggled in interviews, usually coming across quite awkwardly, and rarely able to convey his abilities. Together we composed a letter of introduction and sent it to the interviewing faculty shortly before he met with them. We disclosed his diagnosis and spelled out the specific impressions and concerns an interviewer might have. We acknowledged the environments and tasks that were challenging to my client, and gave specific examples of how he successfully navigated these arenas. We highlighted his traits that would fit well with the graduate program. He was ultimately accepted, his informed professors became his supporters, and he graduated with honors.

Sharing your diagnosis at work can be especially anxiety-provoking since in addition to the emotional energy it takes, there are potential practical and financial consequences. Again, get clear on your goals before disclosing and be prepared to explain the practical relevance of this information. If you are hoping the disclosure helps coworkers or a supervisor understand you better, state that explicitly. If you want accommodations or new procedures put into place to improve your performance, make clear that your goal is increased productivity.

Barbara Bissonnette (2013: 13), author of *Asperger's Syndrome Workplace Survival Guide*, advises disclosing in a solution-focused way, and points out the "making a general statement, such as I have Asperger's and can't multitask" puts the burden of figuring out an accommodation on the people who know the least about what you need.

The impact of diagnosis – disintegration of a false self

Now what? Having obtained a formal diagnosis, you enter a new developmental stage that evokes a shift in your identity. It is a time of both crisis and opportunity.

A diagnosis of autism casts your entire life in a different light. You begin to understand why you may have never felt like you fit in. You may be relieved to understand the source of emotional and interpersonal struggles. You can now begin to better accommodate your idiosyncrasies and challenges. As you learn to accept them (and yourself), you can begin a process of letting go of past tendencies toward self-blame and shame.

Initial reactions, however, can include a cascade of painful feelings, frequently including sadness, grief, anger, and resentment. A pervasive sense of loss may haunt you. You may wonder how your life would have been different if you had realized your autism earlier. You may believe that you were deprived of opportunities and that your potential was lost along the way. You may fear it can never be recovered.

Specific childhood memories may emerge, often of times when you felt excluded, misunderstood, or mistreated. Recalling these early experiences may evoke deep sorrow.

You may long for the chance to erase these early incidents even as you realize you can never go back and rewrite history. You may be tempted to speak with those in your past who teased or bullied you. You may want to punish them or have them apologize. While you certainly have the right to an actual face-to-face meeting, it may not achieve these goals. Others may simply not fully appreciate how damaging your experience has been.

On the other hand, talking with a wise, trusted friend or a professional experienced with autism can be quite valuable during the time immediately following diagnosis. You can safely sort through the memories and emotions rising within you. You may be guided to imagine or role-play a healing conversation in the room with your therapist. You can soften particularly acute memories by writing them down in a letter that you can then burn or shred in a symbolic "letting go" process.

An imagined or role-played conversation with your younger self might also focus on forgiving misguided adaptations, self-imposed negative labels, and internalized shame. To avoid being your own worst enemy, it is vital that your current self befriends your younger unknowing self that still resides within you.

It is likely that a false self-image has developed over years as a result of "faking it" so long you're not even sure who you really are. Trying to fit in may have involved disowning your true beliefs and preferences. Life after diagnosis involves reexamination of your core values.

Your continual need to adapt to the neuro-typical world may have resulted in compromising important parts of yourself. Recognize that it was a trade-off. Yes, you pretended and you were often exhausted as a result. But the alternative may have been a total breakdown.

Self-identification may also involve letting go of a long-standing self-perception of your "specialness." How do you reconcile your unique gifts – which may have been a mixed blessing all these years – if they are part of a "syndrome"? Of course they are still gifts and a diagnosis in no way diminishes them.

Anger may also enter your life during this period. Many newly diagnosed adults struggle with resentment and bitterness. *Why didn't someone recognize what I was struggling with?* You may find yourself enraged when considering how different things might have been with an earlier diagnosis.

Others, including misguided professionals, may advise premature forgiveness. This can actually prolong your fury instead of helping. It is important to allow, acknowledge, and fully experience all of your feelings. Moving into a new self-identity after diagnosis is a process, not an event. This takes time, and evolves in unpredictable ways. Do not accept anyone else's definition of how or when you should "move on."

Adjusting to your new self-identity is more difficult if done in isolation from others. You deserve lots of support while you are developing your new identity. Reading memoirs and online blogs is highly recommended as a first step. Attending at least a few group meetings, if available in your locality, should also be considered. While you may be quite reluctant to meet with strangers, you may be surprised to find others who describe histories and experiences eerily similar to yours.

The next step: transforming your self-identity (the fifth degree of autism)

As your false self continues to disintegrate, and your post-diagnosis emotions begin to diminish, you will notice more focus on your future instead of your past. Your judgment of your history may mellow and memories may become more inclusive – painful incidents now sharing space with times of achievement or pleasure.

Having more accurate knowledge about yourself and having confidence in the evaluation you obtained creates space for musing about new opportunities and lifestyle options. In the past, without this information and lacking professional validation, you may have asked if it was even worth it to continue struggling. Now, with a more solid foundation, a sense of having reached a tipping point usually emerges. Moving forward becomes easier and staying in the past is what takes effort.

One of your tasks during this phase is to determine your needs going forward. An examination of all the areas of your life: emotional, social, family, employment, housing, financial, and spiritual, are these in order? You've already discovered that your internal world is changing. Your external environment may similarly require shifts to better match your new identity.

Consultation with advisors can be very useful at this phase. Having a diagnosis is not the end point, it is an important validation of your experience, a source of additional information, and the beginning of transformed self-identity.

References

Allik, H., Larsson, J. O., & Smedie, H. (2006). Sleep patterns of school-aged children with Asperger syndrome or high-functioning autism. *Journal of Autism Developmental Disorders, July 36*(5): 585–595.

Aspects of Aspergers. (2010). *What it's like to receive an Asperger diagnosis as an adult*. Retrieved from aspectsofaspergers. wordpress.com/2010/12/20/what-its-like-to-receive-an-asperger-diagnosis-as-an-adult/

Attwood, T. (2013, October 16). *Personal email*.

Baio, J. (Eds.). (2014, March 28). Prevalence of autism spectrum disorder among children aged 8 years. National Center on Birth Defects and Developmental Disabilities, CDC. *Surveillance Summaries Center for Disease Control and Prevention*, 63(SS02): 1–21.

Baron-Cohen S., Scott, F. J., Allison, C., Williams, J., Bolton, P., Matthews, F. E., & Brayne, C. (2009). Prevalence of autism-spectrum conditions: UK school-based population study. *British Journal of Psychiatry, 194*: 500–509.

Bissonnette, B. (2013). *Asperger's syndrome workplace survival guide: A neurotypical's guide to success*. London: Jessica Kingsley Publishers.

Crane, L., Goddard, L., & Pring, L. (2009). Sensory processing in adults with autism spectrum disorders. *Autism 13*(3): 215–228. doi: 10.1177/1362361309103794.

Frith, Uta. (2013). *Professional Interview Series*. Retrieved from http://taniaannmarshall.wordpress.com

Gould, J., & Ashton-Smith, J. (2011). Missed diagnosis or misdiagnosis? Girls and women on the autism spectrum. Good Autism Practice *12*(1), 34–41.

Heinrichs, R., & Smith Myles, B. (2003). *Perfect targets: Asperger syndrome and bullying. Practical solutions for surviving the social world*. Shawnee Mission, KS: Autism Asperger Publishing Company.

Hofvander, B., Delorme, R., Chaste, P., Nydén, A., Wentz, E., Ståhlberg, O., . . . Leboyer, M. (2009). Psychiatric and psychosocial problems in adults with normal-intelligence autism spectrum disorders. *BMC Psychiatry, 9*: 35.

Kim, C. (2013). Hiding in plain sight: Diagnosis barriers for autistic women and girls. *Autism Women's Network Contributing Writer*. http://autismwomensnetwork.org/hiding-in-plain-sight-diagnosis-barriers-for-autistic-women-and-girls/

Tani, P., Lindberg, N., Nieminen-von Wendt, T., von Wendt, L., Alanko, L., . . . Porkka-Heiskanen, T. (2003). Insomnia is a frequent finding in adults with Asperger syndrome. *BMC Psychiatry, 3*: 12.

7

The fifth degree of autism

Consideration of all options

Stephen Shore

Introduction

The route from fourth degree autism to fifth degree autism is a landscape of opportunity and a road full of pitfalls and open caverns. It's a journey that requires our previous self-identity to undergo maximum change, which needs research, support, and consultation as well as researching accommodations.

Multiple crossroads and decision points will be made where self-reflection is critical each step of the way. We will stumble into dangers of misinformation and some will confront the option of suicide. We will struggle to see ourselves as either gifted or impaired, or somewhere in between. Will our decisions lead us to a place where we can be a contribution to society or will we ultimately become a societal burden? Will the choices we make lead us from fifth degree autism to sixth degree autism? Having a mentor or guide who understands this key transition point is vital.

The hypothesis for fifth degree autism

Having come this far and gaining a sense of self-identity one might think he or she has arrived. However, the word "commencement" may be more appropriate, as in reality this is just the beginning of your true (new) life. This is the time when you will battle with unique challenges that those of us living as autistic individuals fear and feel the most. This is because we are encountering "change" from all angles.

Sometimes this change hits us like a ton of bricks. For example, I remember feeling queasy while browsing in a used bookstore with a friend when the immensity of what being on the autism spectrum meant to me and how my interpretation of the world was rapidly changing.

Change is one of those concepts that causes major difficulty for us. Mostly, this is because we have problems with forward thinking. If it's planning an outcome from our venture involving our particular interest or passion, we have an uncanny "way" of appreciating the end product. In addition, change brings about a certain amount of unpredictability requiring the processing of novel information from the environment in real time. The sensory issues many of us face results in having to slog through unreliable data from our surroundings. It's a bit like preparing for the day's weather without having the benefit of an accurate forecast.

But, if it's anticipating outcomes from changing relationships, changing social situations, changes to our personal routines, established environments (emotional, work, family, and so on), these cause immense fear, confusion, and pain. This is mentally and physically exhausting. We are torn between wishing we didn't know the truth so we could slip back into ignorance, a place where we didn't have to be responsible for making appropriate choices, or of moving forward in our newly discovered identity. Retreating is as difficult as moving on. Once the light has gone on, there is no returning to the shadows.

For example, after regaling my events of the day to my wife at the end of the day I would then go off to nerd into my computer or engage in other activities. Often she would get mad but I did not understand why. However, continued research into "appropriate" social interaction between couples revealed to me that I needed to reciprocate the data dump of my day that I foisted upon my wife with a request for how her day went *and having to actively listen and provide feedback just as she had done for me* even if I would rather do something else. Often I would wish that I had never learned this social nicety. However, the realization that part of being in a relationship meant *sharing* and not just one-sided data dumping would take over. Perhaps this is part of the reason we are now headed toward our 25th wedding anniversary!

We now need to work to transform our new self-identity. In many ways it's an identity that has been with us all along. But it became marred, buried beneath the weight of societal expectation and our own decisions to conform. The transformation we are now undergoing is a bit like that of the pupa who will become the butterfly. Twice I have gone through phase 5 with the second trip being done much more mindfully. With the benefit of early diagnoses at age two and a half, coupled with my parents openly using the word "autism," since age five and a half I knew I had autism. However, it was not until I reexamined how autism affected me during my struggles toward the end of a doctoral degree in music did I begin to develop an understanding of what it meant to me to be on the autism spectrum.

It takes lots of time and energy to grow into the wonderful individual you were meant to be. It's a process of death in order for there to be life. As an example I am reminded of Winter. At times when I'm cold in the Winter and feel the "greyness" of a particularly drab day, I remind myself that without Winter there would be no Spring.

So, I'm faced with many options. This is a very uncomfortable place to be. Choice is tough for autistic individuals because the unknown is very scary but we so often are not able to "picture" what the outcome of a choice might be.

Options

Our "false" identity worked so well for many of us, or did it? Maybe it got us places we felt we needed to go? But, this constant nagging that somehow this wasn't the real "you" was always there in the stillness of the night or in the moments just after waking. If we filled these times with activity or with clutter we were able to silence that voice. But, now these tools are not so effective.

My "false" identity was great – as a person who *thought* he understood others well and did well in academics. However, part of my integrating a true understanding of how autism affected me meant tearing down the wall blocking reality and engaging in intensive study in areas where I faced challenges. For example, upon realizing that nonverbal interaction was an entire channel of communication that was often more important than the spoken word, I was driven to spend hour upon hour in stores reading books on body language and relationships in a desperate attempt to "catch" up to neurotypical proficiency in these areas. However, this impossible game of catch-up evolved into a realization that while I could possibly reach near expert knowledge on nonverbal communication, practicing it in real time would remain a challenge. At least I realized that it would be a challenge!

Academics, on the other hand, was easier for me to process than relationships. At first accepting that I would have to change my course of study from music education to special education was very challenging as it meant changing all I was preparing to do for a career as a public school music teacher or professor. However, my disclosure of being on the autism spectrum during the application process to a doctorate in special education gave me a fresh start of sorts. My newly forming identity as a scholar in special education with all the differences from being on the autism spectrum, coupled with my professors and advisor knowing the same, helped greatly in adjusting to this new program of study. Additionally, as my understanding grew about my own perceptual, processing, and demonstration of mastery of subject material, I found a world of resources helping me to self-accommodate for my learning differences.

Perhaps we are not used to "sitting" with discomfort. In the past each time we were faced with this emotion we covered it with something that appeased it. For example, when we wanted to flap our hands and we were told this wasn't acceptable we learnt to put them into our pockets instead. When it was painful and overwhelming to look into the eyes of another and someone told us we needed to look or others would consider us dishonest, not interested, or not very bright, we faced the pain and worked hard to look. We spent so many years learning how to fit in. Now, for some of us the reality of the sham is unbearable. We have the option to opt out. Suicide seems much less painful. We could go to sleep and never have to face the reality of our discovery, the discovery of our true self.

But, we are stronger than this. After all it's strength and courage that we needed the first time around, and we need to call on these again. It's an amazing feeling when one defies the odds and stands up for truth and what we know to be right. I'm reminded of the scene from the film *Dead Poet's Society* when the sacked teacher comes into the room and the students defy the authority of the class teacher with them at that time, to stand on their desks and chant "Captain, my captain." This was a very hard thing to do. But, they knew, despite it meaning a public display that put them at risk of school disciplinary action, it was RIGHT.

You do have options. No one needs to face this alone. For each of us, gaining a diagnosis and working on uncovering who we really are is a job that needs the support of others. We can try to go it alone, of course, but this is a bit like the blind leading the blind. There are others who have gone before you. They can help iron out the bumps. If we search the Internet for local support groups, local agencies who understand autism, we will find that they will have names and numbers to share with us to enable the gaining of support.

At times this can be a bit hit and miss, a bit of trial and error. Not every individual you meet will click with you or be able to appreciate your experience. Not every counselor or psychologist is well versed in autism. You will need to try people on until you find the right fit. I know this in itself can be a pain and so many times I was disappointed and felt like giving up. Please, even though you feel like this, keep exploring. It can make such a difference to one's life when we find the right support.

Finding the right people for support is vital, and it's not necessary that they have experience with autism. For example, one of my most helpful mentors while I was a professor of music at a community college was the dean of business. His kind, friendly, understanding manner made him approachable and he was always ready to help me understand the political aspects of the school. It was only when I gave him a copy of my autobiography, *Beyond the Wall: Personal Experiences with Autism and Asperger Syndrome*, that he fully understood I was on the autism spectrum.

Many years later, I am now a clinical assistant professor of special education with a focus on autism at Adelphi University. My being on the autism spectrum is fully known by the search committee. I made this clear when I applied for the position; therefore, it was and continues to be much easier to integrate my authentic self at work and in the community.

Some individuals have tried a variety of therapies too. Cognitive behavioral therapy (CBT) works well for some. In contrast to psychoanalysis where the focus is on finding the root causes of emotional difficulties, CBT takes the experiences of the individual and works on ways to move the person beyond them. For example:

Activating event/action	Beliefs	Consequences	Challenge	New belief
Lost my job	I'm hopeless	Give up	Why should I keep this job?	I'm worth more

For others, ACT or Acceptance and Commitment Therapy:

is one of the recent mindfulness-based behaviour therapies shown to be effective with a diverse range of clinical conditions. In contrast to the assumption of 'healthy normality' of Western psychology, ACT assumes that the psychological processes of a normal human mind are often destructive and create psychological suffering. Symptom reduction is not a goal of ACT, based on the view that ongoing attempts to get rid of 'symptoms' can create clinical disorders in the first place. Russell Harris provides an overview of ACT against a background of the suffering generated by experiential avoidance and emotional control. A case study illustrates the six core principles of developing psychological flexibility; defusion, acceptance, contact with the present moment, the observing self, values, and committed action.

(Harris, 2006: 2)

I found ACT very helpful because it assisted me to accept the past, not pass judgment, live in the now, and build the firm foundation I needed for the future. None of us can change our past and living in regret or disdain only hurts us. It does nothing to build us up or establish us in our newfound identities.

Personality

Then there's our personality style. This is an aspect of "you" that is established over time, is mostly part of your DNA and is an important framework for understanding how you tick. One personality assessment offers some ideas of how personality is composed (the Big Personality Test). It takes us on a journey of discovery that explains who we are and why we do what we do. An understanding of personality is important because personality also impacts upon how we make choices (see: https://ssl.bbc.co.uk/labuk/experiments/personality/).

Some common personality characteristics

Openness

Openness to experience describes a dimension of personality that distinguishes imaginative, creative people from down-to-earth, conventional people. Open people are intellectually curious, appreciative of art, and sensitive to beauty. They tend to be, compared to closed people, more aware of their feelings. They therefore tend to hold unconventional and individualistic beliefs, although their actions may be conforming (see Agreeableness).

People with low scores on openness to experience tend to have narrow, common interests. They prefer the plain, straightforward, and obvious over the complex, ambiguous, and subtle. They may regard the arts and sciences with suspicion, regarding these endeavors as abstruse or of no practical use. Closed people prefer familiarity over novelty; they are conservative and resistant to change.

Conscientiousness

Conscientiousness concerns the way in which we control, regulate, and direct our impulses. Impulses are not inherently bad; occasionally time constraints require a snap decision, and acting on our first impulse can be an effective response. Also, in times of play rather than work, acting spontaneously and impulsively can be fun. Impulsive individuals can be seen by others as colorful, fun-to-be-with, and zany. Conscientiousness includes the factor known as Need for Achievement (NAch).

The benefits of high conscientiousness are obvious. Conscientious individuals avoid trouble and achieve high levels of success through purposeful planning and persistence. They are also positively regarded by others as intelligent and reliable. On the negative side, they can be compulsive perfectionists and workaholics. Furthermore, extremely conscientious individuals might be regarded as stuffy and boring. Unconscientious people may be criticized for their unreliability, lack of ambition, and failure to stay within the lines, but they will experience many short-lived pleasures and they will never be called stuffy (i.e., dull, boring, unimaginative).

Extraversion

Extraversion (also "extroversion") is marked by pronounced engagement with the external world. Extraverts enjoy being with people, are full of energy, and often experience positive emotions. They tend to be enthusiastic, action-oriented individuals who are likely to say "Yes!" or "Let's go!" to opportunities for excitement. In groups they like to talk, assert themselves, and draw attention to themselves.

Introverts lack the exuberance, energy, and activity levels of extraverts. They tend to be quiet, low-key, deliberate, and less dependent on the social world. Their lack of social involvement should not be interpreted as shyness or depression; introverts simply needs less stimulation than extraverts and more time alone to re-charge their batteries.

Agreeableness

Agreeableness reflects individual differences in concern with cooperation and social harmony. Agreeable individuals value getting along with others. They are therefore considerate, friendly, generous, helpful, and willing to compromise their interests with others'. Agreeable people also have an optimistic view of human nature. They believe people are basically honest, decent, and trustworthy.

Disagreeable individuals place self-interest above getting along with others. They are generally unconcerned with others' well-being, and therefore are unlikely to extend themselves for other people. Sometimes their skepticism about others' motives causes them to be suspicious, unfriendly, and uncooperative.

Agreeableness is obviously advantageous for attaining and maintaining popularity. Agreeable people are better liked than disagreeable people. On the other hand, agreeableness is not useful in situations that require tough or absolute objective decisions. Disagreeable people can make excellent scientists, critics, or soldiers.

Neuroticism

Neuroticism, also known inversely as Emotional Stability, refers to the tendency to experience negative emotions. Those who score high on Neuroticism may experience primarily one specific negative feeling such as anxiety, anger, or depression, but are likely to experience several of these emotions. People high in Neuroticism are emotionally reactive. They respond emotionally to events that would not affect most people, and their reactions tend to be more intense than normal. They are more likely to interpret ordinary situations as threatening, and minor frustrations as hopelessly difficult. Their negative emotional reactions tend to persist for unusually long periods of time, which means they are often in a bad mood. These problems in emotional regulation can diminish a neurotic's ability to think clearly, make decisions, and cope effectively with stress.

At the other end of the scale, individuals who score low in Neuroticism are less easily upset and are less emotionally reactive. They tend to be calm, emotionally stable, and free from persistent negative feelings. Freedom from negative feelings does not mean that low scorers experience a lot of positive feelings; frequency of positive emotions is a component of the Extraversion domain.

Trait Explanations

Openness

You are intellectually curious and appreciative of what you consider beautiful, no matter what others think. Your imagination is vivid and makes you creative.

Conscientiousness

You are random and fun to be around but you can plan and persist when work requires. Depending on the situation, you can make quick decisions or deliberate for longer if necessary.

Extraversion

You are constantly energetic, exuberant, and active. You aim to be the center of attention at social occasions and to assert yourself when in groups. You are someone that says, "Yes!"

Agreeableness

You are extremely easy to get along with. You are considerate, friendly, generous, and helpful and you consider most other people to be thoroughly decent and trustworthy.

Neuroticism

You are generally calm. Although some situations can make you feel emotional, your feelings tend to be warranted.

Knowing

Knowing what type of person you are and where you "fit" on a personality scale is important because it helps us know our limits, forgive our limitations and welcome ourselves, in our entirety. If we waste time wishing we were someone else we will miss the opportunities being who we are brings our way. Our eyes will stay closed and only focused upon all we are not. This isn't healthy and does us no good at all. It's important to strive to be the best self we can be as it's only possible to be a poor imitation of someone else.

For example, I see many on the autism spectrum wishing they could be like Temple Grandin. While it may seem like a noble goal at first glance, it's impossible as she, like everyone else, has unique nature and nurture imprints resulting in individual differences. Focusing on the characteristics an individual has and parlaying strengths into areas of productivity is much more fruitful.

So, having considered the options of:

- Either retreating or moving on
- Living with the courage of our convictions or hiding in the shadows
- The type of counseling and counselor we work with best
- Bemoaning our fate based in the belief of lost time and opportunity or choosing to believe the right time, place, and opportunity for us is now and here
- Working within our particular personality
- The best is still to come rather than life is now over

We can now explore the opportunities that come from a firm foundation and walk with our heads held high, even if our steps are a bit shaky. We do not have to do this on our own and we will choose to link up with others, when and where it's appropriate.

This way we can uncover the types of skills and gifts we have that not only can be useful in taking us where we want to go but are also the beginning stages of blessing the community we are part of and not being a burden to it.

Pathway from fifth degree autism to sixth degree autism

Once we have come to terms with our diagnosis, are exploring options and avenues for support, and are no longer allowing the past to pressure our present and hinder our future, we are on the path that leads from fifth degree autism to sixth degree autism. This will be the growing awareness of building up strong and secure our new identity. It will open doors for us as we cease from struggling and home in on acceptance.

For example, I am more productive and am able to contribute much more to society as I continue to integrate my understanding of what it means to *me* to be on the autism spectrum as it colors all aspects of my life.

Conclusion

Arriving at fifth degree autism has been eventful but in many ways it's been a passive journey leading to uncovering and coming to terms with a label that correctly describes who you are. Moving on to sixth degree autism will require more actioning of the information and understanding you have come to know and embrace. The bulk of the foundation is now laid and you are aware of the necessary tools you'll need to actively work on establishing and firming up your new identity; sixth degree autism will explore the means to action this further. It's all about the process of development and this takes time and energy. But, you are well on your way. The more you put into your journey, the greater meaning it will have.

Reference

Harris, R. (2006). Embracing your demons: An overview of Acceptance and Commitment Therapy. *Psychotherapy in Australia, 12*(4): 2–8.

8

The sixth degree of autism

Resolution to live with autism: the crisis of identity

Altazar Rossiter

All the world's a stage,
And all the men and women merely players;
They have their exits and their entrances,
And one man in his time plays many parts . . .

As You Like It, Act II, Scene VII, William Shakespeare, 1564–1616

Introduction

Concepts of identity are relevant to just about everyone. They underwrite every aspect of human interaction and, contrary to the conventions of our various social systems, they are not fixed. However, exposing this myth triggers anxieties from somewhere beyond the rational. This is quite simply because our conventions of identity are concatenated with a sense of our own existence: destabilizing the former threatens the latter, which in turn plays havoc with our personal equilibrium.

The journey from fourth degree autism to fifth degree autism is the consideration and uncovering of our true identity.

The hypothesis for sixth degree autism in this model: identity alignment

A pre-existing identity framework awaits everyone of us before we are born, before we are conceived even. There are many factors that contribute to this framework, none of which has anything to do with who we are at our essence. Some of the main elements of this structure are as follows:

- Gender stereotypes
- Race
- Family name (or its absence)
- Family status (social standing)
- Location (nationality)
- Consensus beliefs
- Cultural practices

As developing infants we're inducted into the grounding structures of "normality" practiced by those around us. These structures are a kind of scaffolding which supports a picture of reality that we are expected to fit into. Some of us fit easier than others. Some of us find pretending to fit easier than others.

Not fitting is not really an option if we want to survive, and the degree to which you don't fit will be the degree to which you suffer in a social context. So you've either got to fit or pretend you do, sufficiently well to get by. Any inner conflict occasioned through forcing yourself to fit has to be discounted. This is the tyranny of identity alignment. Being different is dangerous.

Identity alignment is an acceptance of the existential structure of the social order you are born into and the process of incorporating this as a validation of your own identity.

Identity alignment is the process of accepting a given framework for your personal expression in life, and adopting that expression as who you are.

Identity alignment is a box to hide in, a prison to hold you, and at the same time it's a passport to freedom. Identity alignment enables you to function in the everyday world with a degree of self-acceptance and a common code for interacting with others.

In aligning with the conventions of identity that seem to be available you create a self-identity that defines you to yourself in the context of your environment and experience. What gets overlooked in this is that the whole process is one of interpretation. That's to say you embark on a process of selective self-expression based on how you make sense, or otherwise, of your situation. You do this by examining your environment, your responses to it, and the responses of your environment to you.

This is a compare-and-contrast procedure that goes on without you realizing it, and which engenders virtually unconscious decisions about who's who and what's what. These decisions can basically be reduced to a succession of internal statements, endless affirmations: . . . "I'm this . . . I'm not that . . . I'm this . . . I'm not that . . . " Once a pattern is established that seems to hang together it informs (*in*-forms) every decision and judgment you make.

It makes no difference whether that pattern is flawed, mistaken, or discordant. If it can be sustained by a repeatable train of thought and feeling, and mapped onto other aspects of your experience it will persist. It generates your reality and you identify yourself through it.

This is all relatively benign until you come across something internally that you recognize as part of you but which doesn't fit the reality you inhabit. The reaction can be severe disgust, anger, fear, or shame. The internal statement then becomes something like "Oh no, I'm like that, and I don't want to be – I can't be!" And then comes "**No one must know!**" It's at this point that you move into the realm of self-rejection and denial (Delusional Emotional Non-Identification Anxiety Logic).

There's a whole bunch of negative logic that can spiral out of control from this point. The greater the difference you perceive between the way you know you are and the external ideal norm, the greater the sense of self-rejection and isolation. This feeds into fears of discovery: being discovered by others; discovering greater and greater divergences in yourself. Observation of the way the world treats others who are different will feed these fears and lead to withdrawal.

A kind of desperation to appear "normal" can develop, which is abnormal in itself, and which somehow communicates itself to others. That can trigger their fears and result in bullying, ridicule, humiliation, exile, and persecution. Pretty soon a self-imposed isolation complex can develop that reduces social contact to an absolute minimum.

What's ironic about all of this is that it's normal in itself. That's not to say it's right, happy, or humane. It's generic and it's in the collective unconscious.

So what if you really are on a different spectrum of human existence to the mainstream? What if there really is something "wrong" with you in conventional terms? I guess you know the answers, and perhaps one of the saddest is that you may find yourself aligning your identity with that conventional concept of wrongness.

Who is anyone?

In absolute terms no one walking the earth knows who she or he is. One of the fundamental questions that we all ask ourselves is *Who am I?* In most of us, that's generally followed by others: *What am I doing here?* and *How did I get here?*

For now it's the primary question – *Who am I?* – that concerns us. And I invite you to venture with me into the somewhat scary (some might say dangerous) territory where the conventions of self-identification are exposed.

With that said it's important to be clear that what you read here, in this essay / chapter at least, is not scientific. It's opinion and interpretation (pretty much like everything else somebody spouts as wisdom), my interpretation, and the way you read it will be your interpretation.

Your interpretation will be derived from all your lived experiences and the way you've internalized those in support of how you see yourself in the world. In short your interpretations inform your self-identity and your self-identity validates your interpretations. This is a self-sustaining feedback loop that grows pretty much out of control anchoring your self-identity in what you perceive as your existential circumstances.

It's my contention that your self-identity obscures your true identity and actually disconnects you from it. That disconnection increases with the degree of inflexibility with which your self-identity is established.

You are not who you think you are

Now here's where I'm going to get a bit metaphysical. You'll no doubt (*know doubt*) have picked up that I make a distinction between self-identity and true identity. The implication is that self-identity is a false identity, but that does not mean I consider it to be valueless or wrong – just false. It's something you pretend to be in order to get along in the world, me too. But it's not who you are. **Therefore it's vital to your sanity that you don't hold onto it too tightly.**

I'm aware that that last statement runs counter to popular belief. However, history presents us with many examples of popular belief actually being the opposite of the truth. So perhaps the cardinal sin is closing your mind, and I'm going to be controversial again here.

Once you decide you actually know something you've closed your mind on that particular subject. You know it and there's therefore no need to explore it further. You can file it away for future reference in the confidence that it's fixed and reliable. You can think of this as a sub-routine constantly running in the background, updating your personal reality database with new discrete items of knowledge. Once you've executed that sub-routine anything that challenges the knowing it has authorized must, by implication, be discounted: your mind is closed.

This is important because it's a kind of default functional modality of the mind that builds an illusion of safety. What you know determines how you relate to the world and yourself. So we're back to considering your relationship with yourself, and that revolves around what you *know* about yourself in relation to your world.

Once it begins to be established your self-identity grows, it develops as you develop. It seems that nothing was there before it was. So the illusion is that it's accompanied you from the beginning. But consider this: where does it exist? Where does your self-identity live in reality? Where is its substance?

Let me offer this for consideration: your self-identity is an idea, a concatenation of ideas actually congealed into an amorphous mass. It comprises reflections and remembered interpretations of your perceptions all stuck together in an attempt to make sense of yourself and your surroundings. In short, it's a mental construct. That's all it is. And the more "data" (for "data" read "interpretations") you feed into this construct the stronger it becomes. It solidifies. It becomes an entity in itself.

Now this is a curious phenomenon. The entity that evolves as your self-identity functions as if it has a life of its own – separate from you. Through the mysteries of the mind and mental functionality it believes in itself. It believes it is you. Its existence is dependent upon holding on to all the interpretations it comprises. And that means, by implication, that your existence is dependent upon all those interpretations hanging together coherently.

As a consequence of this, anything that threatens to de-stabilize your self-identity will trigger survival fear. Anything that suggests a flaw in the mental structure you've created to support your idea of yourself has to be eliminated from your reality.

Most simply this elimination manifests as denial (Delusional Emotional Non-Identification Anxiety Logic). But it also makes enemies of anyone who subscribes to a sense of reality that conflicts radically with the one you inhabit.

Have you ever noticed how trying to disabuse someone of a false idea about themselves (or about you) can provoke them into a rage? That's because the background reality they've defined themselves against may be about to crack. Under the rage is a fear; fear that the ground of their existence is going to crumble beneath them. This is nothing less than the fear of physical death hijacked by the mind. It can be thought of as going something like this . . .

- A key interpretation that my mind has used to make sense of the world it finds itself about to disappear.
- If it does disappear the sense my mind has made of itself cannot be sustained.
- But that sense is part of my mind's concept of reality . . . so reality is collapsing.
- My (mind's) existence is not therefore guaranteed.
- And my mind has convinced itself that its existence is my existence.
- My mind thinks it's who I am. It therefore concludes that the existence of the physical organism is in peril.
- Sound the alarm!

This is the main reason why personal exploration and change is often so challenging. We have to face up to the possibility that everything we think we know about ourselves, about the people in our lives, and about the world we live in may be mistaken.

Taking this a step further will show you that any false identity you adopt will not want to admit the existence of a deeper consciousness that might be who you truly are. Once it's established, your false self-identity will be obsessed with self-preservation and that will rely on keeping any expression of a truer being suppressed.

Opening up to yourself, your truth, your uniqueness, facing into your mistaken interpretations and self-perceptions can be devastating. This is the path of the conscious evolutionary. It is not to be undertaken lightly, yet that's the only way to engage with it. This is also the path that must be walked by anyone whose reality paradigm has disintegrated through a major, albeit involuntary, shift in life situation.

Comfort in convention

Human identity isn't fixed, but convention says it is, and that's one of the problems, because in complying with convention you accept the validation it provides for who you think you are. But your identity is something that you build up yourself. It's a construct that facilitates your interaction with others, and with your environment.

There is a comfort in convention. It provides an illusion of permanence. It relieves the existential angst of not knowing what to do. It saves the bother of thinking for yourself. Compliance confers acceptance and approval. Convention is great, but what does it cost?

The identities we adopt are fabrications and deep inside we know this, because we keep having to squeeze ourselves into the boxes that society provides. If we don't fit into those boxes, we become outcasts. Most of us have to make compromises to avoid that fate, by which I mean we're forced to lie to ourselves about ourselves in order to play the social game. This is easier for some than others. Many people enjoy it and just as many resent it. However, lying to yourself is actually toxic. It sets up internal tensions deep in the unconscious that undermine your self-esteem without you realizing how or why. What you do when you lie to yourself about yourself is deny expression to the essence that you are. This is the root of self-rejection . . . and self-hatred.

Without some awareness of this process it's difficult, if not impossible, to evolve beyond coping strategies that just manage to keep the lid on things. Coping strategies are extremely useful in themselves, and they may be all that can be managed in some instances. But for me they don't go anywhere near far enough. So, if you're still with me here, I'm going to see if I can explain a bit more of the way I understand self-identity operates.

The manner in which we create an identity for ourselves is pretty much obscured entirely by the imperative to create it. You need an identity so you can be catalogued and classified, so you can be referenced and registered, so you can be marked and parked, so you can belong. But just how is that identity pieced together?

What's in a name?

> . . . that which we call a rose
> By any other name would smell as sweet;
> *Romeo and Juliet,* Act II, Scene II, William Shakespeare

The wisdom in these lines from *Romeo and Juliet* is profound, and deeply threatening to the status quo of the social order. It's effectively saying that a rose is not a "rose"; the name of something is not what a thing is, not the essence of its existence. What we call a rose is a wonderful example of the miracle of creation and we call it a rose to distinguish it from all the other miracles.

It's the same for people. We've all got names, but they're just labels of convenience. Your name is not who you are. The clearest evidence of this is the fact that many people have the same name, but it's self-evident that they are not the same person. Nevertheless your name forms a significant part of the identity you inhabit.

Our labels distinguish us from other members of our social order – familial, tribal, national, cultural. They enable us to function as individual units within a wider context. The wider the context the more finely defined the labeling becomes. This is an effect of the similarities between us, which need to be bypassed in order to focus in on a particular individual.

Your name is like a ticket to the play. It gives you permission to attend and occupy a certain defined space within a defined context. That context is the social order – convention. And make no mistake, it's an order. The social order governs how you're allowed to behave and it ostracizes you if you fail to comply. Most of us fail in some way and we live with that knowledge internally – a dangerous private secret.

It has to be a secret because should it become known that we're not like everyone else we know we'll be humiliated and rejected. We only have to look around to see what happens to people who are really different.

Self-discovery

Hopefully you now understand some of the potential complexities of how the mind builds structures; structures that are the scaffolding to support its picture(s) of reality. It's now time to look at what happens when that scaffolding collapses.

One of the curious things about the mind is that it responds to direct instructions literally. So when you make a determination that something has to be kept secret, or that **no one** must know, and accompany this with an emotional charge, the mind goes *Oh right, leave it to me: that will never be revealed*. And because "no one" includes you, whatever it is that you determine no one must know disappears from conscious awareness.

This is quite convenient for sustaining a false self-identity. The fact of any discrepancy between who you are and who you present yourself as is one of those buried secrets. Strangely, though, because that knowledge is in your possession it is still available, though not in a recognizable form. Its ghost haunts the scaffolding that holds up your false self-identity.

That ghost comes out whenever you encounter something that reminds (re-*minds*) you of the original burial process. The secret doesn't show itself but the knowledge that it's there does.

Finding out about yourself is terrifying because your secrets have to come out. Then, everything you allowed yourself to believe about yourself has to be revised. That can be pretty much your whole life story the way you think you know it.

How this comes about is different for everyone, although there are general similarities. You may always have nursed a sense that the way you see the world is not the way most of the people you know see it. You may have had a nagging fear that there's something deeply disturbingly wrong with you that you've never been able to identify, and never wanted to. You may have observed, over a period of years, a build-up of suspicions about yourself that fit a paradigm defined by convention as strange, odd, weird, faulty, abnormal, difficult, useless . . .

And then comes that light-bulb moment, or maybe someone tells you something about yourself that was previously unrecognized – you have a condition that marks you as something other than normal. Suddenly you've got another label.

On the one hand this is great, because at last you know. You're different and you can stop worrying about being such a misfit. The straightjacket of consensus reality can come off. On the other hand this can be a major psychological trauma loaded with dread and despair. Your new label most likely invalidates most of the others that you've signed up to.

Suddenly all the confusion you've experienced throughout your life begins to make sense. It's not a sense that you like, but it's sense. Suddenly the strange reactions of everyone you've interacted with make sense – it's not a sense that you like, but it's sense. Suddenly the scaffolding that's been holding up the picture of reality you've assiduously endeavored to fit into is collapsing. The ground of your reality is crumbling beneath your feet – where can you stand now? You might be free – but what does that really mean? And this is just the beginning.

From this point on you're in strange (and as far as conventional reality is concerned potentially forbidden) territory. You're beyond the bounds of what passes for normality in the everyday social order. There is no way back and the way forward is obscured by the confused panic of the mind as it struggles to maintain its sanity. That fact that that sanity is founded on the false self-identity the mind has generated for itself lurks somewhere in your unconscious compounding the panic. Remember what I said earlier in this chapter?

It's vital for your sanity
that you do not hold on too tightly
to any self-identity you create.

This is the threshold of mental and emotional disintegration. At this point the mind is in meltdown frantically trying to hold itself together – and it can't. It has to let go. Few people can make it through this without some kind of assistance. And there are few who are able to assist effectively.

The only way forward is to abandon everything you thought you knew about yourself and your existence – or at least be prepared to abandon it.

Reality in ruins

Finding yourself in the ruins of your reality is not the end of the world, just the end of the world as you've known it up until then. I'm not going to pretend this is a comfortable place, far from it, and that discomfort needs to be negotiated. You are going to have to revise your self-identity completely, and maybe let it be subject to continual evolution as your understanding of yourself grows.

If your self-identity has just imploded the immediate problem is one of shifting relationships, and unless you have a balanced relationship with yourself, balanced relationships with others are out of the question. Recovering to a place where some kind of balance begins to be achieved can take a long time. How long is really a matter for each individual. So what happens in the ruins?

Strange as it may seem, what happens in the ruins is up to you. It's hardly likely that you'll be in a position to believe that, but it's true. You can stay there and fade away or you can look for a way out.

This is a danger zone, as one of the ways out will obviously be suicide. The despair that can accompany a reality and identity collapse is so intense that there are many who take that path. It would be foolish to make any judgment on this as there is no way that anyone can know for certain the ultimate purpose or value of another human life. It is important to recognize, however, just how serious the situation we're exploring is.

Meanwhile, back in the ruins, if you haven't just given up, you'll be stumbling around blindly. What you need to know is that your self-identity will have had various anchors that enabled personal interactions to function. That's to say the old self-identity was not only sustained by your relationships, your relationships were stabilized by your self-identity. No stable self-identity therefore equals no stable relationships!

You cannot get along in the world without some kind of self-identity. It's what enables you to interact with others via the conventions of society. If you explicitly ignore those conventions, or if you don't have the emotional facility to engage with them as if they're true, life gets very difficult.

Whatever hooks and links that your friends and family tied themselves onto will have evaporated – or if they haven't they're about to. Without those anchors you're adrift. The sense of abandonment and aloneness this induces can be excruciating. The bad news is there's nothing to do but face it. The good news is that this is a milestone on the long journey of self-acceptance. And the key to passing it is to understand that any self-identity that anyone effects is an ephemeral contrivance of convenience. But there may be a few obstacles yet to be navigated.

You may be furious that there's no one there to help you. You may be raging that your family has abandoned you. You may hold resentment toward anyone who supported your old false self-identity (because it was convenient for them to do so). You may be angry with yourself for holding onto your false beliefs about yourself for so long. You may be raging at the world, the universe (your God if you have one) for allowing life to be so challenging, so unfair, so brutal. You may curse the first kiss your father gave your mother that led to your arrival in the body you occupy now. You may have fled from the life you were leading and the pretenses you struggled to maintain. All of this turmoil is relevant, as you have to come to terms with it, yet none of it matters.

What matters is that you are entering the realms of truth. Step by step, as you reach an accommodation with all of the negative experiences of your life you are becoming self-empowered. You cannot change your life experiences, but you can re-assess them, revise the decisions you made about them. You will need to be prepared to discard what you knew so well in terms of right and wrong and consider the gaps in between.

If you find yourself in this kind of situation you need to recognize that it's a path that life is presenting to you. It's still your choice whether to explore it or not. It really is a question of empowerment and if you're willing to risk taking ownership of your uniqueness and valuing it, no matter what the world seems to be telling you.

The principles of acceptance

Taking the path of acceptance makes you an explorer. What you'll be exploring is something that no one else is qualified for – the mystery of your own existence. It requires courage, curiosity, commitment, and responsibility. This exploration has nothing to do with the genetic inheritance from your parents or other ancestors – even if you have a hereditary condition. It's entirely about you as a living miracle.

Here's the rub. The path of acceptance is signposted by rejection. What do I mean by that? I mean that every instance, every experience, every feeling of rejection you have is an indication of the direction you need to take. So you're going to have to make some shifts in your perspective that run counter to mainstream thinking. I've outlined a few principles below that might help you on your way.

The first principle: willingness

You will get absolutely nowhere unless you're willing to change, and this runs deeper than you may imagine. You can never know what you're going to discover about yourself (and therefore have to find acceptance for). But if you're going to embark on the adventure of self-acceptance you have to be willing to do whatever it takes without knowing what that might be. Not easy to hold to, and you will back-slide so you have to accept that too. Rejecting your backsliding and any other tumbles you take will stop you dead.

First and foremost in this category is a willingness to see things differently. That's not different from the way others see things – that's already a given, but different from the way you've seen things up until now. And this is where looking at your experiences of rejection have the most to offer you. Every single experience of rejection that's befallen you has to be understood as something you've taken on, something you've believed about yourself from another's perspective – so it's not real, it's a fabrication. Exploring the realm of rejection alone will bring you to new levels of consciousness.

The second principle: start where you're at

You have to begin the journey with yourself; what you feel and what you believe, no matter how awful it seems. Until you face into yourself, your despair, depression, despondency, confusion, and inner chaos, nothing will change. You can only start from where you are, not from where you want to be.

Neither can you start from the past because you've moved beyond that now. Holding onto the past whether it was joyful or torture is just going to keep you stuck. The past cannot be changed, but your reaction to it can. This can and will test your willingness. You'll need to ask yourself what's the pay-off to you for holding on? What does it change? Who does it hurt?

The third principle: nothing is personal

Even though it may feel deeply so, and people may pick on you, project onto you, humiliate you, nothing is personal. All of the negative actions practiced by humanity on fellow human beings originate in the fears of the perpetrator. It takes years of practice to develop your emotional immune system to a degree where you can recognize this and be at peace with it.

Considering experiences of rejection as symptoms of a misinterpretation of reality is step one here. Step two is to find a way of re-interpreting your experience that values you as a unique individual. Step three is to anchor these new interpretations into your psyche so that they inform your sense of yourself.

This may be the most difficult step, and requires some kind of intervention to help release the effects of residual emotional trauma.

The fourth principle: your existence is a miracle

You've probably been taught to consider miracles as a biblical phenomenon related to visions, voices of Divine guidance, and the spontaneous healing of sickness. Maybe that stuff is true, but the very fact that you're here alive and breathing is a miracle in itself.

That you're reading this text, existing on the third planet orbiting a minor star we call the Sun, located in an outer spiral arm of a huge galaxy, that's one of an unknown number of galaxies, in a cosmos so vast as to be beyond our cognitive ability to conceive, is a manifestation of more miracles than you can count.

The shadow side of this is that you might see yourself as insignificant in the great scheme of things. However, the fact remains that you are a self-aware consciousness able to perceive even your insignificance which is also a miracle. You possess the ability to explore what you're conscious of, and the ability to wonder. Wondering at the vast impersonal nature of the universe will help you to stop seeing yourself as a victim.

The fifth principle: there is nothing wrong with you

This is a plain truth. The idea that there might be something wrong with you is predicated on the notion that there is an ideal specification for a human being that you fail to comply with. This is a complete misapprehension, notwithstanding its currency in human society.

This is not to say that you don't, can't, or shouldn't fit into the cultural norms of rightness, it's rather saying that all norms are fabrications. They have their uses, but one of them is not as a datum point to measure any perceived personal deviance against. Norms are merely averages that provide an indication of what might be expected.

At their crudest norms are generalizations of the one-size-fits-all-kind, at their most sophisticated they're cultural tools for disempowering people through shame and exercising control. They are not suitable for application to conscious human beings.

We know that every human being is a unique assembly of chemicals, cells, and energy. No two are exactly alike (unless they're maybe clones). There are always differences and the range of those differences is enormous.

Your primary objective is simply to come to a place of balance with your differences within yourself. It's a curious fact that once you achieve that the rest of the world will support you – and what's more accept you.

The sixth principle: flexibility

The opposite of flexibility is rigidity. In the world of physical structures rigidity is often equated with strength. Rigid structures stand firm. But they also have a brittle quality; they can shatter. When a rigid structure fails the failure is catastrophic and generally terminal.

This is a metaphor that needs to be applied to the mind, to your thinking and knowledge. Flexibility allows differences to be accommodated. It allows perspectives to shift and understanding to evolve. The more you hold onto fixed ideas about yourself and the world, the more difficult any transition into a place of self-acceptance will be.

The seventh principle: expertise

You are to become an expert on yourself. It's an underlying thread of your life's work, whether you realize this or not. You are the only one qualified for this task and until you take responsibility for it you are potentially the victim of others who will tell you they are.

There are many people who are experts in their fields of knowledge and they all have something valuable to share. So it's worth paying attention to anything that supports you in becoming your own expert. However, it's important that you're prepared to let go of everything that offends your heart, no matter who tells you how good something is for you.

Finally, when all lights go out and you're in your darkest moments, cling to any memory of joy, any feeling of happiness you've ever known. Think of it even if you can't feel it, and focus on it. Weep and scream if you need to but hold onto that sliver of joy.

It's a universal law that energy follows intent; what you focus on is where your energy flows. And what you focus on grows. If you focus on your fear and misery – guess what?

So it doesn't matter how obscure or insignificant the light you can imagine or remember, bring your attention to it as much as you can – and let it go when it slips away as it will. It's important that you don't chase it, but just hold it while you can, let it go and do it again when you can. You're cleaning up habitual thought patterns, a bit like cleaning something physically – rinse and repeat. You're teaching your mind that you're not who it thinks you are. It won't be used to that so don't give yourself a hard time if you can't do much at first. You will also be teaching your mind that it can't know everything and it's not in charge – it will not like either of these and will throw tantrums of resistance that will sometimes just floor you.

Conclusion

The path from sixth degree autism
to seventh degree autism

Get some help. Although this finding and being your true self is something you have to do alone the paradox is that it is virtually impossible to do it on you own. Use anything that works whether it's conventional medicine or unconventional personal process work. As long as anything you resort to is engaged with through a conscious choice, you'll be empowered. There's often more value in trying something and discarding it because it doesn't work for you than in finding the magic potion that transforms you overnight. You'll be accepting your own decisions – and mistakes – and shifting your identity into the bargain.

9

The seventh degree of autism

Acceptance

Wenn B. Lawson

Introduction

When thinking about this chapter I thought of degrees as a measure (e.g., mathematics and degrees of freedom). Then I visualized a pie graph showing degrees as stages.

This chapter explores the seventh degree of autism which is a place of acceptance and commitment. This is not the end of our journey by any means, but it is a very important place to get to and one that is vital to furthering the well-being of individuals with autism.

The hypothesis for this model

Being born on the autism spectrum is the first degree or stage of autism that occurs. Having come to the point of recognizing and journeying through life to get to the point of knowing we have autism; going through assessment and then moving on with our lives, we then need to consider what will happen for us next. It could be that we travel through several other stages and move a further degree toward accepting and welcoming who we are. But, this may take us on quite a journey and be a huge process!

The previous chapters have addressed the stages that have led us to this seventh stage, a further degree toward feeling much more at home in our own skin.

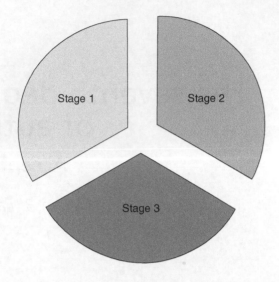

No one expects us to get there overnight but, if we arrive with dignity and respect for the person we are, we have definitely arrived! The person we are is the person we need to be. Hopefully we all change over time to become the person we admire and welcome. But, this is an ongoing process and takes time, support, and our cooperation.

This chapter addresses the issues associated with our newfound identity, in its formalized manner. It will offer an action plan to enable us to move forward in our personal life, vocation, and other branches of who we are, what we do, and what we would like for our future.

The seventh degree

How often do we hear comments like "I've just been put through the tenth degree"? I'm not sure what is really meant by this but it tends to imply that we have gone through "the ringer" and feel thoroughly squeezed of all life. We no longer have any energy or desire to pursue activities or be involved with any type of demand. However, the seventh degree is more about an acceptance of who we are and a commitment to resting there for a while. At this point nothing further is required. The first part to the seventh degree of freedom is to own our captivity. Stop looking for another way out, look your captor in the eye, and own the fact that our autism will be the key that unlocks our future. It is not our prison but our foundation for a way that leads us to Life, with a capital L.

Action 1: accept our label

Acceptance and commitment to our now labeled identity will open doors for us and lead us even further into becoming all we can be. It's not that we are a different person or that much has changed outwardly, but, we now have a different tool set with which to tackle daily life. That tool set emanates from the label of living with autism.

Counter claims to the idea that autism brings ability?

Although this book has shown that autism exists before birth, some will still focus on deficits and impairments. Current patterns being shown by brain imaging technology in individuals with autism are indicating there are reasons for exploring our autistic strengths rather than just areas of difficulties (e.g., Blair, 2006; Dawson, Soulie'res, Morton, & Mottron, 2007; Schneider, 2012). Our interests lead to strengths and are very good tools for enabling success. Success matters.

I believe this is true for all individuals wherever they are on the neuro (autism) spectrum.

Classic autism

Much of the idea that we can grow and develop successfully relates to individuals considered high functioning, previously known as Asperger's Disorder but now addressed beneath the umbrella of high-functioning autism (HFA). Individuals considered lower functioning are also thought of as classically autistic. I dislike these terms because they stigmatize individuals and so often are inaccurate in describing ability and areas of difficulty. I'm using such terminology only to illustrate the scope of the autism spectrum. In my mind these terms translate more into labels like "requiring support, requiring little support, or requiring lots of support."

139

When it comes to achieving a state of self-acceptance for classically autistic individuals, compared to higher-functioning individuals, this process will be different. Classically autistic individuals are often not self-aware and do not live with strong awareness of "other" in ways that allow for connection to social or/and personal attributes. Therefore, self-acceptance may not be an issue for the individual concerned. However, knowing some classically autistic individuals personally I would argue that many are often not as "cognitively challenged" as some might think. Such individuals may not use typical language to communicate, but, once at home with using symbols, pictures, signing, or technology to communicate, they do so very well. This means that they also can access ways to build awareness. Thus, they too will be in a position to build an understanding of "self" and of "other."

If this is the case they will also need support to build a positive self-image. I suggest the way to work on this is by utilizing their strengths, gifts, and interests.

I doubt that statistics showing the degree of individuals attaining self-acceptance exists for this population. In spite of the lack of formal evidence, though, I suggest that individuals with a diagnosis of classic autism can be supported to work to the best of their ability and achieve outcomes far and beyond the expectations of many professionals. Please see: carlysvoice.com/home/aboutcarly/

Why does success matter in autism? It matters because usefulness is associated with value and if we are seen as having value in today's world, we are more likely to feel good about ourselves; more likely to have confidence in those supporting us and more likely to hold our heads up high and walk with dignity and respect. Rather than, for example, paranoia, self-harm, and neglect. With regard to others around us, they are more likely to be accepting of our social ineptness and more accommodating of the difficulties we live with too, if they can see we welcome who we are.

Action 2: believing in ourselves

As we take our place in our own lives and in the lives of those around us it's often our belief in ourselves that lets us down. It's often our dread of social situations and our lack of confidence that prevents us from "faking it to make it." Now, because we know what we are dealing with, there is great hope that this will improve. As our confidence grows we can feel at home in our own skin, hold our heads up high and, at least if we don't feel skilled we can act as if we did. Doing this isn't lying so much as it is following a script that leads us to the outcome we want.

Because we know we don't learn as regular individuals might we also know that we learn, but we learn differently. We need to use this knowledge in applying the right techniques to our chosen supports. Then we can learn the things we need to that enable us in life. The right support, for example, can be the "seeing eye dog" for autism because it can give us "access to the fuller picture" that enables us to have a voice to help us share with others. This may present in the form of technology (e.g., easier to type an email than speak face to face); a social skills program; building up and flexing our emotional and social muscles or by utilizing some other means that allows us to live with confidence. Practice might not make us perfect but it certainly helps.

Some of our best-known brains remain a mystery and yet have given us scientific advances that have changed the lives of thousands. Temple Grandin, a lady currently in her 60s, diagnosed with autism as a young child, is well known for her animal husbandry skills and specific design of cattle chutes; Temple has gained an amazing reputation for her work that is worldwide. Schneider (2012), in his experiments using neuro-feedback from fiber tracking of the brains circuits with Temple, found that her brain shows dramatic disorganization of the part of the brain used in language. Even so, Temple, with her lack of social prowess, is a very successful business woman who has set plans in motion to take care of herself in her elderly seasons of life (personal conversation, April 2012).

Schneider's work is very positive when it comes to exploring autism because it shows very clearly the reasons why language skills in autism can be so difficult to grasp. However, coupled with this knowledge of speech and language difficulties in the brain of individuals with autism is the knowledge that we can communicate very well via other means, not only words. Assistive technology, for example, may be a useful support. It could give some of us the voice we long for. We don't have to stay locked away from communicating our needs, thoughts, and feelings, just because speech is difficult or not accessible. iPads and their many applications (Apps), for example, open doors to communication that many of us couldn't even have imagined. There are Apps for everything!

In the typical population individuals let others know their needs, thoughts, and feelings through the use of language. This is usual. But, allowances are made for individuals who are hard of hearing, have sight and mobility issues and other issues that go with being human. Although we live with these difficulties too, allowances also need to be made for our autism. iPads, PCs, and telephones that utilize the latest technology allowing for assistive software to act as the medium we express our voice through should be available, acceptable, and even mandatory in some institutions of learning. If they are viewed as an individual's "right," just like the need for a walking cane, those working with us will not question the need of such devices for those who choose that form of communication.

Action 3: seeking IT support (low-tech or high-tech)?

So, if you are a member of the population of individuals with autism who are not famous and not so well off, how do you access such technology? I think we need to get in touch with organizations that regularly update their IT equipment. We can let them know of our need for an iPad, laptop, notebook, or desktop computer so they are aware we are prepared to buy second-hand. There is also eBay, local newspapers, the corner shop, word of mouth, local colleges, and charities. The local library in your area also will allow you to use its computers, free of charge, so we can utilize this option too.

It's common knowledge in autism we learn best when our interest is engaged (Lawson, 2011). But, if you are not interested in IT, computers, or some of the means on offer for communicating your own needs, you might prefer old-fashioned pen and paper. Whatever it takes to get across to necessary people what it is that you require from them.

Action 4: self-acceptance

I so often hear the words "self-acceptance." It's as if these words magically make my life easier. I struggled for many years trying to understand what the phrase meant. Then, one day, after years of counseling and lots of work reading on the topic I began to appreciate that self-acceptance was about stopping trying and starting to receive. It was about ceasing to rush around and simply let things be. It meant giving up the fighting, the sorting, the battle, and give in to "surrender." This was not an act of defeat so much as an act of bravery. It was in letting go that I actually could realize what I had.

Accepting myself, warts and all, meant saying that just as I am, I'm OK! I don't have to aim to be a better person. I don't have to acknowledge my failures and try harder. No, this is what I'd been doing all my life and all it achieved was more failure. Instead, simply saying to myself, "Wenn, you are welcome; Wenn, you are created; Wenn, you are loved." No ifs or buts, just the way you are! It released something in me. That something is called "life." This acceptance began the journey for me of further becoming who I wanted to be. This is the beginning though, not the end. It doesn't mean I've arrived at the last stop. But, it lets me move on to the next one rather than continuing to go around in circles.

The impact of awareness upon the individual

It took quite awhile to align my identity with who I truly am. Part of that journey is in finding appropriate support. If we don't feel comfortable with the counselor we see or the support group we are part of, we might need to find another one. Give yourself license to value who you are and treasure yourself. Only submit that treasure to those who also will value it and keep it safe.

Finding ways to sustain self-acceptance and prevent mental health issues is vital. Lots of positive self-talk and choosing well who we relate to, share ourselves with and associate with, is so important. Sometimes our own families can be toxic. If this is the case learn to be polite and engage socially in what you feel is your duty, but please don't submit your soul. It will be trampled upon and not treasured.

Spending time doing the things you enjoy is also very important to finding a place of accepting self. Time with what interests us gives us a sense of value, it boosts motivation and a sense of well-being. I often wonder how many of us, as individuals with autism, ever reach this stage? To what degree do we own who we are and welcome ourselves? I don't think there is a simple answer to this question because life doesn't deliver us a straight course to run. Rather, it comes with many junctions, roundabouts, hills and valleys too. What we gain on the roundabouts we are in danger of losing on the swings. So, to help sustain our personal growth we might do well to stay longer on the ride that helps maintain momentum and be less quick to swap for what appears to offer a greater thrill!

Part of self-acceptance is owning we are not typical

Someone once asked me if I would take a "cure" for my autism if there was one. I said "No." I am not sick, I don't need medicine for my autism. Suggesting I need to be cured implies I'm not OK with being autistic. It also implies that being typical is superior and it's not. I know many typical individuals who live with a variety of difficulties and these go with being human. If I were born with a typical brain it does not mean I'm immune to problems. So, being typical will not fix me, because I'm not broken.

We are often said to lack empathy, but, actually I find we are often over-empathetic and this means we turn away from situations that require our attention. For example, when a person is sick or needy we may not be able to cope with that person's demand. Not because we don't care but because the person's discomfort is overwhelming for us. At times it's difficult for us to show empathy because we don't experience a connection to the person or event that requires empathy. It's very interesting to see how this can change, though, once we find a mutual point of connection.

Living with autism may mean we are totally unaware of the age differences that exist between us and others. I know I find it very difficult to tell another person's age and this can mean I'm insecure about how to relate to them. Giving me a way to check this out would be great as well as letting me know what kinds of behavior go with particular ages.

Younger autistic females may get very anxious, just like males with autism; however, for some, their anxiety is rarely physical or disruptive in their younger years. They develop great coping mechanisms as younger females often turning their anxiety inward to depression and paranoia. It's as if it just isn't "lady like" to tantrum! Not having legitimate expression for their anxiety builds up over time and, during menopause in particular, the walls crumble and they can no longer hold it altogether. It's better to acknowledge and not bury the things we battle with. It might be in a letter or an email to myself. It might be in a spoken thought? Whatever way works for us is the way to go.

For some of us it's not in our personality to make a fuss. We may once have been described as shy, quiet, solitary, or loners. For us it will be very difficult coming to terms with the changes we are experiencing as our physical bodies age. This is true for most of us whether typically or autistically developing. But, if you are a member of the generic population you have access to a variety of resources to help you through this transition. Finding alternative ways to support our aging if we can't ring a friend for a chat, meet up for a cuppa, or share our thoughts and feelings is very important to ongoing mental health. Sometimes we are our own best friend. I like talking to myself and sorting out the bits that need sorting. I like to write and draw too. Finding a healthy outlet for our emotions is a good idea. Some of my friends use video games or television programs. Find what works for you then use it.

Males with autism don't go through menopause, but they may face physical differences that impact upon sexual libido, muscle tone, and loss of head or/and body hair. These changes can be suddenly noticed rather than grow slowly with the individual. Such shock can cause panic and a variety of stress support needs that no one can explain because they don't realize what is happening for that person.

Some other noticeable differences between individuals are just that, individual issues. Some individuals like very "girly" or feminine pursuits while others, even though they are female, may be inclined to less feminine activities. It's the same for the guys. Being male does not always mean you will like beer and footy! Whatever your gender, you are an individual and will need others in your life to take the time to get to know you.

Just because we need support with ordinary things it doesn't mean we aren't capable. I can write a PhD thesis and speak in front of hundreds of people. But, I often depend upon friends and family to help with the everyday demand of typical life. Everything from budgeting my finances, getting the shopping done, sorting out my personal, educational, and leisure time activities, domestic chores, and sometimes even personal hygiene, are all things we may need support with.

However, for each of us to attain the seventh degree of autism we need to accept our diagnosis and work on commitment to our becoming happy, whatever it takes, with who we are.

Action 5: environmental support

We are much more than the sum of our thoughts, however. For some of us the benefits of fresh air, living in a quiet neighborhood, having proximity to green fields and nature, as well as being part of an accepting community are vital to maintaining a healthy state of well-being.

To avoid predators, we need to feel good about who we are. I remember always walking while looking at my feet. I avoided eye contact with other people and rarely help my head up in public. This unhealthy stature sends a message to others that I am vulnerable. This is not a good message for would-be predators! One day a friend said to me "Hold your head up high, Wenn, you have done nothing to be ashamed of." I started to practice walking with my head up. I didn't look directly at people though so much as in their general direction. It was amazing! Something magical happened. I began to notice that passers-by smiled at me, spoke to me or in some other way, acknowledged me. This hadn't happened to me before.

I liked the way their acknowledgment made me feel. It boosted my confidence and this in turn helped me cope better with being among people. It didn't take my sensory issues away so I still had to wear ear plugs to cope with noise in busy environments and I still needed my shades and/or Irlen lenses to enable me to cope with light. But, it did wonders for my feelings of positive self-worth.

Action 6: exercise

Another contributor to my feelings of positive self-worth is exercise. Although exercise seems like something we may take for granted, it's often under-estimated in its value. Exercise is the one thing we can do to help us in so many domains. It lowers blood pressure, helps us burn unwanted fat, helps deter decay in our cognitive functioning, helps to prevent diabetes, and promotes a sense of well-being.

Unless I have a reason, I am not comfortable with going outside. I do not own a dog so I can't take "my" dog for a walk. I don't cycle outside, mostly because my knees are not physically stable. I don't like sport or walking for its own sake. But, I do like using my exercise bike parked in front of the television or computer and I can "work out" while watching a favorite show. This way I get my exercise and I'm happy to do it.

It might be that we are happy relating to a Wii or some other activity? There is a way to happily exercise, we just have to find it.

Gender identity

The little girl dressed in Pink,
A little boy in blue.
The ethics here are clear you see,
They sing the human clue.
The picture of what's right.
The picture of what's wrong.
We see it everyday, we see it every way.
We hear it in a song.

But whose song do we sing?
Who do we represent?
All of humanity or just the ones we get?
What's the guiding rule here?
What's the thing to do?
The rule is: It's different, it's different for me and for you.

Gender identity is another aspect of who we are. But, it isn't always clear cut. Traditionally males have been more frequently diagnosed than women. Thus, if you are a woman with autism you might doubt your diagnosis; feel even more of a misfit and be more likely to head toward mental health problems. Please take heart. You are not alone.

It is widely believed that many more females exist who would qualify for a diagnosis of autism than previously thought. When we look at the gender ratio it is more likely to be pretty equal, especially when intelligent quotient (IQ) and developmental quotient (DQ) are factored in (Fombonne, 2003; Worley et al., 2011). This means when we remove some of the obstacles related to IQ and DQ, the gender ratios diminish and males and females look more alike, with regard to their autism, than they might otherwise appear.

On the issue of gender, some of us experience gender confusion very early, expressing a desire to be the opposite gender. Yes, this may be a "special interest" in children but it's unlikely to only be an interest if it persists into later life.

Generally we think of women as being more socially inclined than men. This can put extra pressure on autistic females because it says "If you are female you should be able to . . ." This type of thinking isn't helpful. Let's accept we may have difficulties in this area and work slowly and consistently toward lessening them. There is no finishing line here but an ongoing moving toward being more confident and more at home with ourselves.

Action 7: sensory dysphoria

Our senses are the first port of call for all information. But, when one's senses are delivering an over- or underwhelming stimulus, behavior that follows can seem strange (covering of ears, rocking, spinning, humming, sucking, and so on). I accept I live with senses that are easily overwhelmed. This is me. So, I can take care of myself by wearing shades if I need to; headphones, if that's what it takes; sometimes I need my cap and sometimes I need to stay home.

Accepting that I live with sensory issues is an active part of accepting myself. I don't need to apologize for this part of me, just accommodate it. I can let friends know in advance what works for me so they won't be disappointed or upset when I'm sensory-overwhelmed. Instead we can plan for this and, hopefully, avoid it.

Action 8: coping with change

Most of us like our routines and we all have preference for certain things. Whether it's a favorite mug or TV program. The difficulty for us is it's extra hard to let go of what we know because we find it difficult to forward think and imagine our life without that. It's OK to feel uncomfortable, to sit with the feeling and acknowledge it. But, we need a plan to compensate. So, if plan A might not happen we can explore plan B or plan C.

Being at home in the social world and using language to share in social events is common practice in the typically developing world. If, however, socializing, knowing how to address others appropriately, using social conversation and understanding "small talk" is an issue for us, we may need to do some homework on this.

Take it on as a subject to study and work on. Being better equipped in this domain will help us build confidence and feel better about ourselves. Change happens in many ways so many times. Being prepared for it, whether it's in conversation, expectation, or whether it sneaks up on us in other ways, I find it helpful to accept that changes happen. One of the most helpful expressions that I have learnt is the "oh well." It doesn't explain anything or take me to a place or space I prefer, it just acknowledges that something happened and it's uncomfortable but "oh well," it happens.

Action 9: interests

It's pretty common in autism that we tend to have some particular interests. We focus upon one interest at any one time and are not wired up to switch quickly between interests. On the one hand this is great news for working with one particular skill set, one thing at a time, but, it's not so good when others want us to join their interests (unless we are interested)! So, making the most of what interests us is a good thing. Also, letting others know of our difficulty with switching between interests is important so they know not to take it personally.

This doesn't seem to be different according to which gender you are either. It seems to present equally in both. Our interests are our ticket to the kind of vocation we may want. I know I have difficulty with social situations, being in the outside world, and in general being involved with "small talk" or superficial gatherings. But, I'm good at other things and have some particular skills that stand me in good stead for my working life. I love to write, to teach, and to research topics of interest to me. I can use these qualities to enable me to earn a living and contribute to my sense of self in a healthy way. Our passions may be the pointer we've been looking for!

Summary: our tool set

Acceptance of our label and of ourselves
Counseling and support by named others
Commitment to uncovering who we are
Self-belief in all we are and can be

Environmental support (e.g., diet, exercise, time with nature)
Gender acceptance in all its diversity
Our passions and interests that can take us where we want to go.

Conclusion

In many ways there is no conclusion to this chapter because it's part of an ongoing process. **Moving from the seventh degree to the eighth degree is the next part of this process.** However, this ongoing process begins and ends with us. We can't blame anyone else for our journey. We might have been given a great start in life, we might have had a more bumpy ride. But, if we recognize where we are today, we already have the skills to begin exploring what we can do to take us further along the road we are choosing to travel. This is our life and we are responsible for our decisions. Others may have left us wounded and bleeding, it's up to us to pick ourselves up, brush ourselves off, and carry on.

References

Blair, C. (2006). How similar are fluid cognition and general intelligence? A developmental neuroscience perspective on fluid cognition as an aspect of human cognitive ability. *Behavioral and Brain Sciences, 29*, 109–125.

Dawson, M., Soulie'res, I., Morton, A. G., & Mottron, L. (2007). The level and nature of autistic intelligence. *Psychological Science, 18*(8): 657–662.

Fombonne, E. (2003). Epidemiological surveys of autism and other pervasive developmental disorders: An update. *Journal of Autism and Developmental Disorders, 33*, 365–382.

Lawson, W. (2011). *The passionate mind: How individuals with autism learn.* London: Jessica Kingsley Publishers.

Schneider, W. (2012). *Walt Schneider Lab.* Retrieved from http://schneiderlab.lrdc.pitt.edu/content/60-minutes-20120716

Worley, J.A., Matson, J.L., Mahan, S., Kozlowski, A.M., & Neal, D. (2011). Stability of symptoms of autism spectrum disorders in toddlers: An examination using the Baby and Infant Screen for Children with Autism-Part 1 (BISCUIT). *Developmental Neuro-rehabilitation, 14*(1), 36–40.

10

The eighth degree of autism

Unconditional service

Sara Heath

Introduction

Life's journey with autism consists of many stages, and on attaining the seventh degree of autism we now have the foundation for stepping up to the eighth degree of autism. This is where self-acceptance and identity alignment combine to empower the autistic individual forward. This gives more self-confidence in his or her abilities, but still with skills to learn and practice, and many issues needing to be acknowledged. The autistic individual starts to create and later accept a place in society, where he or she can use his or her skills and receive acknowledgment for them. So eighth degree autism is more than a promise, it's now on the horizon.

Hypothesis for the eighth degree of autism

As the autistic individual applies his or her gifts to benefit others he or she is rewarded for the service. This enables the individual to integrate fully into the community where his or her gifts are perceived as benefiting the locale. This is an exciting period because, at last, the individual's skills and abilities are recognized and valued giving rise to feelings of gratitude and compassion.

Therefore, autistic individuals gain a sense of well-being which is enhanced through unconditional service which in turn supports the feeling of being valued by society. If this transpires to international recognition, the individual is on his or her way to ninth degree autism.

When an autistic individual embarks upon the eighth degree of autism this furthers acceptance and healing. However, there are also many challenges to come to terms with during this stage. Many people, especially those late to be diagnosed with autism, may be backward looking and still often haunted by problems from the past. Accepting that they are past problems, even if unresolved, they belong in the past and, as such, need no longer hurt us. In eighth degree autism we can let go of previous hurts and trauma, either done to us or by us, accept our unique but special difference from others, and look gently forward to the future. This is where autistic people can explore skills they have and seek to use these positively. Making a difference in theirs and other's lives, they become an accepted part of the community.

Some examples of life in the eighth degree

The late Dr. Danny Beath was proud and pleased to have autism. Danny sadly died in 2012. He was a botanist but also a naturalist, having studied Botany as an undergraduate he then achieved a doctorate in Tropical Ecology. As his preferred medium for communication was visual, Danny was rarely seen without his camera. He then used his skills to become an esteemed, award-winning photographer. Danny was also accepting that his autism meant he had a different use of language. Danny used many analogies as this was an important way to express how he felt; he therefore painted pictures with words.

Danny studied plant life and then became fascinated by the insects that visited the plants. He especially loved butterflies as he had seen many rare species in the rain forests of Africa and South America during his studies. He also loved the British butterflies that he photographed during the summer months and loved to talk about these stunning creatures.

Danny often described himself as "a blue butterfly in a field of Meadow Browns" as he knew the life cycle of this butterfly (which was unique). Danny was highly aware that blue butterflies show up more distinctly than brown ones. They stand out, but are then preyed upon more than the brown ones, who are camouflaged by their color.

Danny knew a great deal about being preyed upon as he had been bullied a great deal as a young person. Blue butterflies are also beautiful, and, in his opinion, much more attractive than the "boring brown ones." Being blue – even silver-studded blue – they stood out as he did. Danny was proud that he stood out. He was not afraid to be different, standing out as he often did when he wore his typical brightly colored tie-dye T-shirts. He was not embarrassed or ashamed that he had autism.

It was Danny who helped and inspired many others with autism to come to terms with their issues and to use the skills and talents that autism often brings. He had lived experience and great compassion for fellow members of the autistic community. For many of his mentees, his support and inspiration has enabled them to gain employment, or at least to live a fulfilling and contributory life in society.

Danny discovered that even though he was dyslexic, with his amazing eye for detail and thorough knowledge of the life cycles of creatures, he could take photographs that others could only dream of. Danny had the patience to wait for the right picture to come, having already foreseen the photograph in his mind. He climbed hills at "silly o'clock" to take photographs of misty valleys at sunrise, or sunset in what he called "Middle Earth" – his beloved county of Shropshire.

Danny soon discovered that he could win local photographic competitions and this lead him to winning national ones as well. Winning gave him structure, purpose, great focus, and improved self-esteem. He became even more proud to have autism, as he was aware that it was his difference that gave him such extraordinary ability.

There are many other individuals who understand their gifts are due to their different wiring, and that autism does not have to be disabling. Isabel Stone is an extraordinary and published poet, able to describe in bejeweled terms the pictures that she sees. Each poem is unique and perfect, with no error or typos and each poem is a gift to read and enjoy. Eric Loveland Heath is a musician who has autism and who creates unique ambient electronic music. He taught himself to play the guitar and all the other instruments that he uses, and is now a self-employed composer.

A few years ago Eric decided to learn Welsh and released T⬚, a CD written in Welsh purely and simply because he was fascinated by the language of the country so near to his own. Once released, T⬚ was featured on local radio and was then album of the week for several national radio stations. Eric is an inspiration to others. He is compassionate and understanding of others with his condition and has often advocated on behalf of local autistic people.

Victoria Clinton is an extraordinary fine art portrait painter with an amazing eye for detail. She is fascinated by the old masters and paints with oils in that ancient style. Recently Victoria completed a posthumous portrait of Dr. Danny Beath who was very positive about her work. Danny always visited her local exhibitions. Victoria knows that it is her autism that gives her amazing talent. It is her intense focus, her perfectionism, her eye for detail, and her fascination with people's faces that has made her work so exceptional.

Other more famous individuals with autism include Daniel Tammet who also has savant skills, an amazing gift for languages, and a phenomenal memory for numbers. By the way, although many savants are autistic, being autistic does not generally mean that you will be a savant – though you almost certainly will have skills that are unusual in the general population.

Tammet recited pi from memory to 22,514 digits in five hours and nine minutes on March 14, 2004. There are also people who are similarly gifted and are known as "calendrical calculators." One of our Autonomy members, Stuart Jones, is able to work out within seconds after you have given him your birthdate, the day of the week you were born and what was top of the hit parade on that day. Stuart can sing all the lyrics. He can even tell you what the weather was like on that day.

Using your autistic special interests is often a challenge, but can help with a career or improve self-motivation. This can help move you toward ninth degree autism.

Learning to see the flip side

If you are brilliant at memorizing all the characters in Star Wars this might not be thought of as a skill. If this is where you are stuck it could even be thought of as a problem and a hindrance when developing a career. But many autistic people are great at spotting the faults (what I call Autistic Virus Checkers) so you will often see the gaps or potential that others miss. Autistic individuals can be extremely good writers and many can hide their less positive autism traits when they act. Acting via scripts can be a life skill and a camouflage some have needed and have developed over many years! Some are brilliant mimics. I remember Danny telling how he wound his father up as a youngster. He would make sounds of a faulty motor! Danny used this skill to put animals and birds at their ease by mimicking their songs and cries when he took amazing photographs of them in their natural environment.

Lifestyle management

An important key to success as an autistic person is self-understanding. This means being aware of our strengths and weaknesses, and knowing our limitations. Being positive about autism might mean being aware of future possibilities. It also involves being realistic about the issues that are faced in getting there. A common problem for people who have intellectually high-functioning autism is exceeding their stress threshold. This can cause periods of depression and times of feeling very down.

One autistic individual described his low moods as "the long dark night of the soul." Negative thoughts can often cloud the minds of autistic individuals. This is due to the fact that life has been extremely challenging. It's important that when these thoughts occur you do not let them take over and pull you down. Finding ways to accept, channel, and manage this is very helpful. Autism is a variable condition with fluctuating capacity so there are often times when you will seriously struggle with motivation and very negative thoughts. Although this can be irritating and frustrating it is usually temporary and not long-lasting.

Danny in particular found it difficult to cope during cold winter months unless he was photographing sunny snow scenes. But he thrived in spring, summer, and autumn when the weather was kinder. Danny's passion to win also affected his motivation when he failed to win first prize, and this would often set him back by several days, but he always bounced back!

The rubber band analogy

Having been taught well by Danny, I often use analogies when coaching and mentoring autistic people. Many of the individuals I work with have had significant problems in their lives and are very late to be diagnosed (most over the age of 40). One analogy I use when supporting a person at this stage in his or her life is the "rubber band" analogy.

When we are younger and more flexible, we all tend to be more "elastic." We can stretch quite thin to cope as a rubber band does, and then it returns to its normal size when the need to stretch has gone. The problem is when the rubber becomes old and worn or stretched too thin, then they snap. Mentally and often physically this happens to us all as well, metaphorically. This is my analogy for severe autistic overload. The constant stretching to cope in mainstream life can mean that the autistic rubber starts to perish and the band gets more rigid and inflexible. Autistic rubber bands that have snapped are never the same again. You can tie a knot in them and they will still work but they will be smaller and will never stretch as thin or as wide as they did before.

In many, as yet undiagnosed, people on the spectrum, there has been a need to cope with so much more than typicals have to manage. This is due to the lack of understanding all around. Therefore, this rubber band overload and melt down is often seen as mental health or psychiatric problems. Stress can show as paranoia or psychosis and many have become so ill they have been hospitalized.

Autistic people, however, are often very resourceful and will find ways to cope with overload, and to stop it happening again. Unfortunately this can include self-medication with alcohol or drugs, self-harming through cutting, self-neglect, disassociation, or extreme obsessive behavior. A more positive way is to accept that overload will happen due to having autism in a world that often doesn't "get" you. Pacing yourself and having quiet time alone, using a special interest and focusing on what nourishes you, is a more positive way to cope and recover.

Another analogy/metaphor I use to explain problems with motivation is the human propensity to make a mountain out of a mole hill. This relates to how many of us "amplify or magnify" the problems we face in life. For autistic individuals especially these are huge and scary, even if not actually seen by others to be real problems. Tony Attwood calls this behavior "catastrophizing" (we do need to appreciate, though, while the problem may not seem real to others, it's very real indeed for the individual). This is then linked with the inflexible, rigid, and uncompromising perfectionism of autism and can lead to a slow down or coming to a full stop. Autism magnification of a mole hill makes it seem so much bigger. It also allows the small imperfections and flaws to show up in more detail than normally is the case.

This is where the skills of perfectionism can actually be a detriment to people with autism, as due to their rigidity of thought there is no point doing something unless it is perfect.

On another note such autism perfectionism can be very satisfying and is often therapeutic too. It can bring control back to people's often chaotic lives. This does, however, link with time management problems as well, as perfection takes time and effort. Danny struggled in this area but was also very skilled at using photo editing software to remove flaws and imperfections, even deep into the many layers of the photograph. Danny used the winter months to do this time-consuming but therapeutic work.

Possible limits of being self-employed?

By being self-employed, Danny had to learn to compromise. He had to learn that being perfect costs too much at times so he learnt to accept some minor flaws. He learnt to conform, to fit in even though it did not make sense to him to do so. Danny's daily battle against what he called "mediocrity" is the same as others with autism. This clearly describes the problems others with autism have in gaining the motivation to succeed because they have such high expectations for success that they do not readily accept failure.

Many will see this as rejection, with a reaffirmation of their failure with relationship issues, partnerships, and even childhood friendships, colored by a past tinged with bullying and loneliness. Danny's memories of school were being an "outsider," never joining in and "always, always being left out of other children's games."

An analogy that Danny used was more positive; he likened himself to an eight-cylinder motor – a Porsche motor. He explained that a motor of that size takes a lot of power to get going, to be firing on all cylinders. This needs a lot of energy and motivation. The large motor analogy explains how difficult it is for some autistic people to get motivated, started, or to make the first move. But once up and running they can power themselves through the tasks in hand. Then, it may take a long time to stop, as their proverbial engine is so hot and fired up. I am aware that many autistic people actually have a very slow stopping speed – which is another way of explaining their difficulties when coping with or processing change. They are "still traveling" when other more typical people have put their brakes on.

My own analogy for gaining motivation is that of the steam train, from Thomas the Tank Engine stories. Steam engines do not work when cold and need a long slow build-up but a few hours. Once the engine is "full of steam," set it on the track and it will travel at high speed for some hours, but like the Porche motor, will take many more hours to cool down.

Danny used to say that as a Porche he would easily travel down a motorway at high speed, but was not good at all when driving around the small and narrow town center. His analogy for mainstream people was that they were typical one-liter cars which were good at getting around town – i.e., socializing with others, and dealing with mundane things in life – but lacking his skill and focus they would never overtake him on the "motorway of life."

Metaphor for life

When a task is too big, and autistic people have made a mountain out of a mole hill, then several strategies can be put in place. One of them is acceptance that they will magnify tasks in this way due to their autism. Another is accepting that rigidity and inflexibility are the main cause for many issues. Here is another analogy – in Shropshire we have some beautiful hill country. When you look at a mountain you do not always see the paths up it, but they are definitely there. When you find the paths you know there is a way up the hill, and you have a solution to the problem. The way up every mountain is via a path, and autistic people need to look for and identify the path. This is often difficult due to decision-making issues (e.g., how do you know if it is the right path, how do you know how steep it will be? How do you choose the right path from all of the others?).

In this stage we break the tasks down into the small components because magnifying everything makes them look far too big and scary. But as we all know the journey of 1,000 miles starts with the first step. When we start to climb a hill – or start on a task that we are not really motivated to achieve – it seems tough and we can't always see the top or the end result. If we take our first steps up the hill – or do 10 minutes on the task – and after 10 minutes turn around and look back we can see the distance we have traveled. This will motivate us to go farther. That's how mountains are climbed, one step at a time.

One of my useful coaching tips is "just do 10 minutes." So often when you start a task, even if it is not climbing a hill, and do it for 10 minutes you forget about the time and find you have achieved it 30 minutes later!

A further problem for us all is that autism presents many communication issues. When autistic individuals are so single-minded and focused on one thing, it's very difficult to see the bigger picture which requires more than single attention. This gives the impression to others that autistics lack imagination or find it difficult to see another person's point of view. It is therefore essential for the non-autistic person to understand the problem is often theirs, not the other way around. Typical people need to have an understanding that autistic people are not meaning to be difficult when they do not understand, if they can't visualize it they don't get it!

If they feel they will fail they may well also refuse to do a task. So sometimes an incomplete task may not be done due to a lack of motivation but more a lack of understanding or a clear systematic view or explanation of what they are expected to do. This is what I call the importance of "sequential clarity" when working with autistic people.

I often ask at a training session for individuals to tell me how to boil an egg. So how do you boil an egg? The problem is that even typical people would not be able to answer this question as it is much too vague. Typical people seem to cope with a lack of clarity and will try to answer the question, but when we get into the specifics then even a typical person would be unmotivated to cook an egg without clear instructions; autistic people are therefore no different.

Autistic people need to know the right way to complete a task as they do not like to compromise. As you are aware boiling an egg depends on the size of the egg, the temperature of the egg at the time, how you want it cooked – these factors dictate how long you cook it for. If it is explained to you in a clear and uncomplicated way that it is a small egg, at room temperature, and you want it hard-boiled, then the task for autistic people and their typical peers becomes much easier.

I was once asked a question if autism is 95% ability or 95% disability. I answered that it depends on the stress level of the task in hand. In my opinion if the stress level is low and the task is interesting and motivating, then autism becomes 95% ability, only 5% disability. However, if the stress level is high and the person with autism is finding the task is unmotivating, uninteresting, and demoralizing, this then has a link to possible failure. Then the autism becomes 95% disability and only 5% ability. This then shows that it is not a task that is the problem or autism that is the problem – it is a combination of both. The issues of motivation, concentration, and needing things to be perfect are high on the autism list. Accepting this as a part of having autism is important as you travel forward on your self- realization journey.

Ongoing autism support

Even when autistic people have come to terms with the condition and are well into the eighth degree, they will still suffer when their rubber bands begin to wear, and will often feel very negative and low. There are several different forms of support that the successful autistic individual may benefit from. However, these are not always easy to access and some of them are costly.

For those who are not in work, and sadly most autistic people are not in full employment, joining a self-help or social group is often the cheapest way to gain support and friendship from other people. Most local councils have a list of these groups, and they are also often known to the National Autistic Society. Danny found the Autonomy group extremely beneficial. He could support others, teach them about photography, and also have a good time talking about his amazing and varied interests, with the addition of several pints of real ale.

Others can join online forums and network on autism-specific sites and there are many sites on the Internet; there are even autism-specific dating sites.

Some autistic people may decide to have counseling where they can talk through challenging issues and learn from them. This is often a time-limited and free service via your GP (in the UK), but with often a long waiting list. Others are subsidized but whatever type you choose, it is very important to let the counselor know that you have autism. Most counseling, especially if the counselor uses Cognitive Behavior Therapy (CBT) which is designed for mainstream people, will need to be adapted for the learning style of autistic people.

Others may choose life coaching and if they are fortunate enough they may even be able to find an autism coach who can help them to move on further in their lives. Reaching specific attainable goals is so important. All of the counseling centers I know of are private but many will arrange flexible and non-face-to-face ways of support, e.g., phone, Skype, texting, or emailing.

Some others are trying alternative support by exploring the use of meditation and Mindfulness, attending sessions in Neuro-Linguistic Programming (NLP), having massages of different types, and having lessons in the Alexander Technique.

A further choice can be to try prescription medication to help alleviate depression and anxiety. Professor Michael Fitzgerald says,

Antidepressants (and other forms of medication) can support self-acceptance if used responsibly and in low quantity. These meds work by reducing anxiety and helping to manage depression. Autistic people should continue taking medication as long as they benefit from it. Sometimes medication works very well for autistic people, though some individuals react with idiosyncrasy. Therefore, it is necessary to find a unique combination of medication and therapy that suits the individual.

The path to recognition (the ninth degree of autism)

The path to the ninth degree of autism is based upon active service to help others. This transformation is supported by realizing one's potential fully and passionately applying your gifts with an open heart. The key to success is being aware of our gifts and finding a way to apply them for the benefit of humanity. Isobel communicates through her vivid poetry; Victoria, Eric, and Stuart communicate through art, music, and maths, but are also trainers in autism awareness; they show and demonstrate their skills which help professionals understand more about autism. This in turn will help others with autism be supported better by those professionals.

As we have seen with Danny, he became so adept at photography that he won national and international competitions and awards; his style of photographs was often recognized as "a Danny" photo and he too was an autism trainer and advocate when he spoke at events and conferences.

As such our eighth degree autistic individuals begin to spread their "blue butterfly" wings, are proud to stand out from the Meadow Browns, and are recognized for their difference and because they are different. These autistic people will then be in great demand as they progress from eighth to ninth degree autism.

11

The ninth degree of autism

Recognition, mastery, and unity

Temple Grandin and Debra Moore

What a man can be, he must be.
This need we call self-actualization.

Abraham Maslow[1]

Introduction

The ninth degree of autism is reached when we have achieved self-mastery, made a positive contribution to our environment, and gained a sense of unity with the larger world. It is important to acknowledge that this is very aligned with Maslow's hierarchy of needs, and is not unique to those with autism. Those on the autism spectrum, however, usually must overcome significant barriers to achievement of this level, and deserve tremendous respect for the journey and this hard-earned attainment.

Hypothesis

As a person on the spectrum moves through the developmental journey of recognizing the role of autism in his or her life, there are usually many obstacles, crises of confidence, and periodic setbacks. From the initial dawning awareness of being "different" and the emergence of both emotional and physical reactions, a need for confirmation and recognition of our struggles often becomes pressing. At this point, either through self-identification or formal diagnosis, the beginning of a new identity germinates. While frequently accompanied by a sense of relief at finally beginning to understand past struggles, this period is also often marked by confusion, ambivalence, and a sense of being overwhelmed by how to incorporate this new sense of self into daily life. With support, resolution to accept and integrate the autistic parts of oneself grows. Self-acceptance often blossoms into a strong focus on these parts, sometimes accompanied by a commitment to involvement in the autistic community. This can take the form of extensive reading, participation in online communities, support groups, or even becoming a recognized speaker or writer about autism. At this point one's autism may be the dominant vehicle by which service to others and to society is delivered.

The ninth degree of the developmental trajectory of autism continues this movement into an increasingly complex, nuanced, and personal actualization. Grounded in awareness and acceptance of one's autism, this period adds greater appreciation of all parts of oneself. Autism no longer defines our entire being – it is simply a label that helps highlight both struggles to be cognizant of, and unique gifts to be treasured. Life goes on within the awareness of our common humanity, no matter what our personal neurological wiring.

Components of recognition, mastery, and unity

As one achieves the ninth level of autism, perspectives about oneself and the world have solidified into a healthy, positive outlook. The basic assumption about oneself is that capability and achievement are possible. Any remnants of a "deficit model" of thinking have been eliminated by this stage of the autism journey.

Whereas earlier in the development of our identity, we may have thought our self unable to change or to find our place in the world, we have by now gone through many stages of evolution and experienced an increased sense of self-mastery. Whereas we may have frequently hidden from the world (or at least the world outside the autism community), we now invite that world into our own life. We are curious and want to absorb diverse parts of life.

A necessary component of reaching the ninth level of autism is self-accountability. We're all tempted to make excuses at times, and to avoid difficult or awkward situations. At the ninth level we recognize when this is happening and move forward in spite of anxiety or frustration. We realize compromise is positive and necessary and do not begrudge that not everyone is like us.

We are willing to tolerate change as necessary, as well as ambiguity. We are able to see the gray in life and not rely or insist on unimportant, rigid rules or dogma. We do not seek to create emotional drama in our lives, but instead actively seek cooperation and collaboration. We remain open to the opinions of others because we realize their perspective may have value. At the same time, we are willing to voice and advocate for our own beliefs, even if it creates discomfort in ourselves or others.

At this point on our developmental trajectory, we reject a sense of entitlement. We recognize that we share both differences and similarities with others, both in our neurological wiring and our personalities, whether those people are on the autism spectrum or not. We do not use our differences as excuses, but we also do not discount them.

We seek to continually work to remove or minimize obstacles to our self-actualization. We recognize self-sabotage when it occurs. We have acknowledged former bad habits and sought support for making changes. We have organized our lives to enhance our physical, mental, and emotional health. We take care of the basics such as getting sufficient sleep, and making healthy dietary choices.

We align ourselves with others who are positive in outlook and actions. We choose interpersonal interactions carefully and selectively and seek out others who are also making sound choices in their personal and professional lives. The ninth degree of autism brings a sense of peace with oneself that is often missing from earlier stages.

The vital importance of "fit"

An important feature of those who have reached the ninth level of autism is that they have achieved what we call "fit." This concept assumes that each autistic person is unique. We have specific, individual ways of processing and remembering information. Our interests and passions are unique and not necessarily shared by others. Additionally, temperaments and personalities can vary widely within the autism spectrum. Each of these unique qualities must align with a person's environment in order to achieve optimal "fit."

Recognizing these unique qualities allows a person to maximize his or her strengths and work around or minimize challenges. This has huge implications for finding success in one's personal life, relationships, and career choices. A striking limitation of current diagnostic methods is the focus on simple "in or out of the box" thinking – pronouncing "yes" you are autistic, or "no" you do not fit diagnostic criteria. We need more specific and comprehensive assessment tools that provide feedback on how we think and process information, what our unique strengths and challenges are, and how we can find a "good fit environment." The profiles of those who have achieved ninth level autism that follow below often have this in common – they have either stumbled onto or deliberately created good fits for themselves.

Temple acknowledges that in 1995, when she originally described her own visual thinking, she assumed all autistic people were like her.[2] Later, however, "after reading a review on Amazon.com – which I admit really stung, I needed to further reflect."[3] This led to the hypothesis of additional thinking styles that encompass the diversity of those with autism.

The scientific research shows that there really are two types of visual spatial thinking: one type involves thinking in pictures and the other in patterns.[4]

Thus, the three types of thinking are as follows:

1. Photo Realistic Visual Thinkers
2. Pattern Mathematical Thinkers
3. Word Thinkers

Photo realistic visual thinkers automatically see concrete pictures in their mind. When they reproduce the picture it contains detail and tends to be precise. Vocationally, they are well suited to find good fit in the arts, design sectors such as jewelry and crafts, industrial automation, graphic design, or landscaping. They are also good candidates for technicians who work with concrete parts of things, such as cars, or machines. They can spot visual errors efficiently and accurately. In relationships, they can remember interactions and occasions by seeing details of a scene or object. They can bring superior skill (and tremendous savings) to companies or organizations by being able to visually anticipate design flaws.

Pattern mathematical thinkers can see and manipulate patterns in a way far superior to the general population. Reaching the ninth degree of autism for this type of thinker may include making a positive contribution in fields such as physics, engineering, math, and computer programming. In relationships, their ninth degree of autism may reveal itself in the ability to recognize patterns in verbal or visual interactions. They may bring superior skill to organizations by spotting faulty theory and they can find patterns in what others perceive as randomness or chaos. Silicon Valley and other geographic hubs of technical innovation often are full of largely unrecognized ninth degree autistics. "Techies" in these arenas may have the best of both worlds – good fit in their specific jobs, and also in their overall work environment, surrounded by "their people."[5] Increasingly technology companies are recognizing the unique talents of people formally diagnosed and are seeking them out.

Word thinkers are good at writing and manipulating words and letters. Their ninth degree of autism often manifests in positive contributions involving organizing and structuring. They often make superior journalists, translators, and researchers. Interpersonally, they bring gifts of excellent planning and arranging. Partners and friends may appreciate that they carefully arrange activities and environments.

No matter which thinking style describes them, most people on the autism spectrum, whether low or high functioning, have poor short-term working memory.[6] Rote memorization of data or patterns, and long-term memory may, however, be above average. Realizing and factoring into your personal and professional life both the strengths and challenges of your memory has significant bearing on finding a good fit and satisfaction in the ninth degree of autism.

The ninth degree of autism in one's professional and personal life

It would be a mistake to assess whether someone has reached the ninth degree of autism only on the basis of vocational or professional results. Our culture tends to over-emphasize skills that are exhibited in public, or that receive popular acclaim. In today's world many people, especially members of generations X, Y, and Z place personal stock in the number of their Facebook "likes" or Twitter followers. Baby boomers may value titles, awards, and accolades. But those who have reached the ninth degree of autism may never procure public recognition or renown. Their positive contributions may be local or even within their circle of friends and family. Their personal integrity and the healthy integration of autism into their overall life may be simply reflected in their ordinary daily actions.

Women on the autism spectrum often reach the ninth degree of development via less recognized routes. While many autistic women have achieved high vocational or professional status and have made exceptional and conspicuous contributions to our world, there are many others who have bestowed equally valuable contributions in more private ways. Mothers on the autistic spectrum (whether employed outside the home or not) who have achieved self-awareness and have learned to highlight their strengths often bring amazing gifts to their children and their communities. Volunteers who open a child's eyes to possibilities, who bring dignity to the marginalized and overlooked, or who simply bear witness to and accompany another person during a painful crisis are often functioning on a ninth degree foundation.

Examples of ninth degree achievement*

Charlie Devnet, tour guide[7]

For the past 10 years, I have worked at a historical house museum. I love my work for so many reasons. First of all, the site itself is both peaceful and inspiring. My colleagues have provided me with a sense of camaraderie. One of the best aspects of my job is that it allows me to talk. For two and a quarter hours, visitors must follow me around and listen to me speak about matters in which I am interested and knowledgeable. A guide has to be comfortable with public speaking, which presented me with a great challenge. In my first year, I was criticized and I came very close to losing my job.

During that first summer, my mother died, and her loss threatened to send me into a serious tailspin. I needed the structure and the socialization that my job provided, and I acquired the social skills that were necessary to keep it. By dint of sheer self-will, I developed enough skills to hang on to my job. I discovered in myself abilities that had lain dormant all my life.

When talking about career success, if you're referring to fame and fortune, a fat paycheck, a position of power, or a world-shattering discovery, I have nothing to offer. The personal level of success and fulfillment I have found is invaluable. Today, guests often compliment me – sometimes to management – on what a knowledgeable, funny, and articulate tour guide I am. I have never become exactly like the other guides here, but in my eyes I've managed to become something even more meaningful. I've finally become myself.

Grant Manier, artist[8]

At a very young age, Grant developed a passion for paper, and by his early teens began collecting and recycling as an affordable way to continue his passion. He is emerging as an intriguing and captivating young artist whose eco-friendly artwork is capturing the attention of his community and the national media. He has been honored with numerous awards both for his art and his contribution to the autism and special needs community.

In his own words from his website:

I am an author, artist, and special needs advocate. I have autism and I have daily challenges and struggles, but my disability has become my ABILITY to contribute to help changing the earth's environment and raise the awareness of special talents among those with different abilities. It's not what I can't do . . . It's what I can do that makes the difference!

Anita Lesko, nurse anesthetist, military aviation photojournalist, author, and Asperger's group facilitator[9]

My specialty is anesthesia for neurosurgery. There is a tremendous amount of detail to tend to. It all has to be planned very carefully. I thrive on all the detail!

Organic chemistry was my best subject in school. This is where I discovered I'm a visual thinker. I am able to see the chemical structure in my mind, as if on a huge movie screen. I could mentally manipulate them into whatever shape was necessary.

I am also an internationally published military aviation photojournalist and flew in fighter jets and helicopters. This all began when I saw "Top Gun" and my special-interest laser like focus took over.

I also started an Asperger's support group and began speaking publicly at universities, schools and hospitals.

The single most life-changing event for me was writing my book.[10] It showed me all the things I have accomplished in my lifetime, and I accomplished them not knowing that I had Asperger's syndrome. Oh, it wasn't easy by any means – but I never gave up. Perseverance became my middle name. When I completed my book it enabled me to be the hope and inspiration for others. I believe they too can achieve their dreams by thinking positively and believing in themselves.

Neal McRaw, veterinary surgeon in Scotland[11]

My current profession is as a general veterinary surgeon in a rural practice. During university, despite feeling that I was in the wrong profession, I stuck it out and earned my degree, with some difficulty. Then, slowly, a rather wonderful thing happened. I started to gain a deep satisfaction from my work and realized that I was, in fact, at least reasonably good at it. I came to feel a deep affinity with my patients, especially dogs and cattle, and I developed an ability to interact reasonably well with their owners.

Until recently, my likes have perforce been solitary activities – reading, long-distance hiking, and studying – as I was unable to break through the autistic barrier between myself and the outside world. Recently, however, I have at last been able to enjoy the pleasure of interacting with small groups of people. I love the Scottish Gaelic language, which I have learned as a second language. When I was young, I loved and learned to play the Highland bagpipe, and I still play.

The main challenge I have overcome is finding a way, albeit late in life, to break down the autistic barrier between myself and other people. I cannot express how significant a step forward this has been for me. I have built up a good relationship with the clients and, funnily enough, I have ended up working for and beside two of my fellow students from years ago.

I feel that as my self-knowledge and understanding of my condition has increased slowly over the years, starting in my 40s when I read Tony Attwood's book,[12] my insight into and appreciation of my veterinary work has grown proportionally.

John Elder Robison, mechanic, designer of special effects for rock bands, successful car dealership and repair shop owner, and author[13]

John writes on his website[14] that he was a self-described problem child who was often sad, a loner, unable to make friends, and a high school dropout in 10th grade. After joining a band, his natural insight into electronics led to him designing special effects guitars for KISS. From there, he writes, he made the leap into a job as an engineer at a major toy and game company and moved up the corporate ladder for 10 years until hitting a wall. He was a manager, but miserable, and finally quit. He began fixing Mercedes and Land Rover cars in his driveway, which grew into one of the most successful independent repair businesses in New England, known for restoration and customization.

He attributes a life transformation to being introduced to Asperger's syndrome by a therapist who happened to walk into his repair shop. He published his memoir in 2007, which became a bestseller and launched him into his new calling as a speaker and advocate for people with Asperger's and other forms of autism.

Prominent historical figures who may have achieved the ninth degree of autism

Charles Darwin, scientist

The father of evolutionary theory, Darwin's perseverance and intensely focused passion for collecting things led to profound changes in how we view species and our world. He shared his observations in detailed writing and though his books sparked great debate and criticism at the time, he continued to pursue his dream. His findings have led to innumerable advances in the biological sciences, psychology, and medicine.

His achievements are all the more impressive when we consider that he struggled in other academic areas – a common discrepancy found in autism. He was unable to learn a second language, felt perceived by others as below average in intellect, and did poorly at Cambridge University.[15]

Albert Einstein, scientist

This theoretical physicist and philosopher of science developed the theory of relativity in reaction to his perception of flaws in Newtonian mechanics, which at the time was accepted without question. He shared his findings in over 300 scientific papers and over 150 non-scientific works. His findings have contributed to advances in countless fields including quantum physics, engineering, cosmology, and mathematics.

Einstein did poorly academically until allowed to attend a school that let him use his superior visualization skills. Beginning there, his visual thinking, which let him see patterns that were missed by others, eventually led not only to theoretical paradigm shifts but also to the eventual development of many of our modern technologies. He once stated, "Thoughts did not come in any verbal formulation. I rarely think in words at all. A thought comes, and I try to express it in words afterwards."[16] It has also been written that Einstein silently repeated words to himself until age seven.[17] This may have been what is referred to as silent echolalia, a common autistic trait.

Vincent van Gogh, artist

One of the best-known post-Impressionistic painters, van Gogh was known for his vibrant colors and intense, turbulent patterns. Nevertheless, during his childhood numerous developmental delays were present. By definition, autism has an early onset with common traits appearing. Like Einstein and Darwin, van Gogh showed no early superior skills, and in fact threw many tantrums and was a loner as a child.

In 2006, physicists compared van Gogh's patterns of turbulence with the mathematical formula for turbulence in liquids. Note that his paintings date to the 1880s, while the formula dates to the 1930s. Yet the artist's turbulence in his paintings (think *Starry Night*) provided an almost identical match for turbulence in liquid.[18]

Summary

The ninth degree of autism is marked by recognition, mastery, and unity. Recognition does not imply public commendation, but instead reflects a positive self-awareness of autism and authentic, informed recognition of both its challenges and gifts. Mastery is defined as manifest knowledge, skill, or proficiency in an area of passion and meaning. Unity refers to the achievement of integrating autism into our professional and personal life in a manner that neither dismisses nor dominates who we are. Unity also involves interconnection with others, including those not on the autism spectrum.

By the time we arrive at the ninth degree of the autism developmental journey, a sense of peace has grown within us. We realize what is most important is not what is in our past, or what labels we may carry, but who we have become.

Notes

* While some contributors in this book have probably achieved the ninth degree of autism, we decided for maximum objectivity to only include profiles of people who did not participate in its writing.

1 Maslow, Abraham. (1943). A Theory of Human Motivation. *Psychological Review*, no. 4 (1943), 370–396.

2 Grandin, Temple. *Thinking in Pictures*. New York: Doubleday, 1995.

3 Grandin, Temple, and Panek, Richard. *The Autistic Brain: Thinking Across the Spectrum*. Boston: Houghton Mifflin Harcourt, 2013.

4 Kozhevnikov, Maria, et al. Spatial vs. Object Visualizers: A New Characterization of Visual Cognitive Style. *Memory and Cognition*, no. 33 (2005), 701–726; Kozhevnikov, Maria. Creativity, Visualization Abilities, and Visual Cognitive Style. *British Journal of Educational Psychology*, no. 83 (2013), 196–209; Mazard, Angelique, et al., A PET Meta-analysis of Object and Spatial Mental Imagery. *European Journal of Cognitive Psychology*, 16, no. 5 (2004), 673–695.

5 Grandin, Temple. *Different . . . Not Less*. Arlington, TX: Future Horizons, 2012.

6 Grandin, Temple, and Duffy, Kate. *Developing Talents*. Shawnee Mission, KS: Autism Asperger Publishing Co., 2004.

7 Devnet, Charlie, condensed, as quoted in *Different . . . Not Less*. Arlington, TX: Future Horizons, 2012. Temple Grandin, Editor.

8 Retrieved from www.grantsecoart.com

9 Lesko, Anita, condensed, as quoted in *Different . . . Not Less*. Arlington, TX: Future Horizons, 2012. Temple Grandin, Editor.

10 Lesko, Anita. *Asperger's Syndrome: When Life Hands You Lemons, Make Lemonade*. Bloomington, IN: iUniverse, 2011.

11 McRaw, Neal, condensed, as quoted in *Different . . . Not Less*. Arlington, TX: Future Horizons, 2012. Temple Grandin, Editor.

12 Attwood, Tony. *Asperger's Syndrome: A Guide for Parents and Professionals*. London: Jessica Kingsley Publishers, 1998.

13 Robison, John Elder. *Look Me in the Eye: My Life with Asperger's*. New York: Crown Publishers, 2007; Robison, John Elder. *Be Different: My Adventures with Asperger's and My Advice for Fellow Aspergians, Misfits, Families, and Teachers*. New York: Random House, 2011; Robison, John Elder. *Raising Cubby: A Father and Son's Adventures with Asperger's, Trains, Tractors, and High Explosives*. New York: Random House, 2013.

14 Retrieved from www.johnrobison.com

15 Grant, A. *Charles Darwin*. New York: Appleton, 1885, as quoted in Grandin, Temple. *Thinking in Pictures*. New York: Random House, 1995.

16 Highfield, R., and Garter, P. *The Private Lives of Albert Einstein*. New York: 1993, as quoted in Grandin, Temple. *Thinking in Pictures*. New York: Random House, 1995.

17 Patten, Bernard M. Visually Mediated Thinking: A Report of the Case of Albert Einstein. *Journal of Learning Disabilities*, August–September, 1973, No.7.11.

18 Aragon, J.L. Turbulent Luminance in Impassioned van Gogh Paintings. *Journal of Mathematical Imaging and Vision*, 30, no. 3 (March 2008), 275–283, as quoted in Grandin, Temple, and Panek, Richard. *The Autistic Brain: Thinking Across the Spectrum*. Boston: Houghton Mifflin Harcourt, 2013.

Further Reading

Beardon, L., & Edmonds, G. (Eds) (2008). *Asperger Syndrome and Employment.* London: Jessica Kingsley Publishers.

Beardon, L., & Edmonds, G. (Eds) (2008). *Asperger Syndrome and Social Relationships.* London: Jessica Kingsley Publishers.

Beardon, L., & Worton, D. (Eds) (2011). *Aspies on Mental Health.* London: Jessica Kingsley Publishers.

Edmonds, G., & Worton, D. (2005). *The Asperger Love Guide.* London: Lucky Duck. Foreword by Luke Beardon.

Edmonds, G., & Worton, D. (2006). *The Asperger Personal Guide.* London: Lucky Duck. Foreword by Luke Beardon.

Edmonds, G., & Worton, D. (2006). *The Asperger Social Guide.* London: Lucky Duck. Foreword by Luke Beardon.

Edmonds, G., & Beardon, L. (Eds) (2008). *Asperger's Syndrome and Social Relationships.* London: Jessica Kingsley Publishers.

Lawson, W. (2011). *The Passionate Mind: How Individuals with Autism Learn.* London: Jessica Kingsley Publishers.

Wylie, P. (2014). *Very Late Diagnosis of Asperger Syndrome: Autism Spectrum Disorder.* London: Jessica Kingsley Publishers.

Websites

http://minicolumn.org/people/casanova/
http://www.bild.org.uk/our-services/journals/gap/
www.wennlawson.com

Index

Page numbers in italic format indicate figures and tables.